FabJob Guide

# Become a Boutique Owner

DEBBRA MIKAELSEN

# FABJOB® GUIDE TO BECOME A BOUTIQUE OWNER
## by Debbra Mikaelsen

ISBN: 978-1-894638-87-6

Library and Archives Canada Cataloguing in Publication

Mikaelsen, Debbra
FabJob guide to become a boutique owner / by Debbra Mikaelsen.

Includes bibliographical references.
ISBN 978-1-894638-87-6

1. Fashion merchandising—Management. 2. Stores, Retail—Management.
3. Fashion merchandising—Vocational guidance.  I. Title.
II. Title: Become a boutique owner.

HF5429.M498 2005   381'.45687'068   C2005-905705-X

**Important Disclaimer:** Although every effort has been made to ensure this guide is free from errors, this publication is sold with the understanding that the authors, editors, and publisher are not responsible for the results of any action taken on the basis of information in this work, nor for any errors or omissions. The publishers, and the authors and editors, expressly disclaim all and any liability to any person, whether a purchaser of this publication or not, in respect of anything and of the consequences of anything done or omitted to be done by any such person in reliance, whether whole or partial, upon the whole or any part of the contents of this publication. If expert advice is required, services of a competent professional person should be sought.

**About the Websites Mentioned in this Guide:** Although we aim to provide the information you need within the guide, we have also included a number of websites because readers have told us they appreciate knowing about sources of additional information. (**TIP:** Don't include a period at the end of a web address when you type it into your browser.) Due to the constant development of the Internet, websites can change. Any websites mentioned in this guide are included for the convenience of readers only. We are not responsible for the content of any sites except FabJob.com.

| FabJob Inc. | FabJob Inc. |
|---|---|
| 19 Horizon View Court | 4616 25th Avenue NE, #224 |
| Calgary, Alberta, Canada T3Z 3M5 | Seattle, Washington, USA 98105 |

To order books in bulk, phone 403-949-2039
To arrange a media interview, phone 403-949-4980

# www.FabJob.com
## THE DREAM CAREER EXPERTS

# Contents

# About the Authors

 Guidebook author Debbra Mikaelsen has been a fashion industry consultant for the last eight years, and has been working in fashion design and production since 1986. She has contributed to the success of several boutiques in North America, and has also worked with fashion designers, apparel whole-salers, garment manufacturers, and vertical retailers. For this guidebook she draws on her own experience in the fashion and retailing industries, as well as numerous in-depth interviews with successful boutique owners. Debbra is also a contributing author to the _FabJob Guide to Become a Fashion Designer_. Her freelance writing has been published at the apparel industry website **www.just-style.com** as well as in _International Living_ magazine.

Contributing author Pamela Skillings brings you the bonus material on opening a bridal boutique in this guide. Based in New York City, she provides marketing and business development services to both large and small companies, including boutiques and apparel designers. Prior to launching her consulting business, Skillful Communications,  Pamela worked as a senior marketing executive with both Citigroup and MasterCard International. Pamela is a contributing writer and editor for About, Inc. (**http://manhattan.about.com**). Her articles have also appeared in _The Scarsdale Inquirer_, _Audubon_, and other publications.

Additional material and research for this guide were supplied by FabJob editor Jennifer James and FabJob staff writer Craig Coolahan.

# Acknowledgments

This book could not have been written without the support and expertise of several interviewees who generously shared their time and thoughts about success in retail fashion, strategic pricing and sales techniques. Thank you to the following people whose wit and wisdom, experience and savvy contributed in immeasurable ways to this guide:

- *Elizabeth Andrei*
  Here Comes the Bridesmaid, New York, NY
  **www.bridesmaids.com**

- *Margaret Czeszejko-Sochacka*
  From Seeds To Fashion, Steveston, BC

- *Wendy de Kruyff*
  Dream, Vancouver, BC

- *Jane Hedreen*
  flora & henri inc, Seattle, WA
  **www.florahenri.com**

- *Shane McMurray*
  The Wedding Report
  **www.theweddingreport.com**

- *Beth McTavish & Jacqueline Verkley*
  Halfmoon Yoga Products, Vancouver, BC
  **www.halfmoonyogaprops.com**

- *Beverly Michaelsen*
  The Wandering Wardrobe, Port Townsend, WA
  **www.wanderingwardrobe.com**

- *Sue Papilion*
  Tall Etc. Pasadena, CA
  **www.tallwomen.com**

- *Philip Solman*
  Small Business, Big Brains, Coventry, UK

# 1.  Introduction

Congratulations on taking the first step towards starting up your own boutique, a step into the fast-paced, ever-changing, exciting world of fashion retail. You're about to spend your days surrounded by beautiful clothing, shoes and accessories, and by fun, dynamic people.

Most people who are interested in the idea of owning a boutique have certain things in common, so we think we might already know a little bit about you. Do you love to shop? Do you enjoy the special thrill of hunting for a chic, jazzy little number, or the perfect tie to match your favorite chinos? If so, you probably already spend a lot of time in boutiques, and know what you like and don't like about them.

Perhaps you find yourself unconsciously window-shopping for friends and relatives. Do you see a sweater and think, "Oh, that's Jim!" or are you constantly scoping out handbags that would suit your sister? If so, you'll probably be a natural success at selling in a retail environment, where you'll help people find items that match their style and taste.

Chances are you've spent a bit of time shopping in boutiques and you might possibly have worked in one or two. While it can be fun and rewarding to work in someone else's shop, nothing quite compares to the satisfaction of running your own business, and taking credit for your own ideas and flashes of brilliant customer service. You'll face interesting new challenges as you learn all of the aspects of having your own business. The profit you make will be your own, as will the accolades of the people who become your regular clientele.

One of the keys to running a successful business is being prepared, and this guide is a vital part of your research. It will provide you with concrete guidelines and a few strong opinions. It will let you gain insight from those who have already successfully done exactly what you will set out to do, and who have so generously shared their experiences with us.

So, let's extend to you a warm welcome into the world of the boutique!

## 1.1  Boutiques and Fashion

What is a boutique, anyway? Most people would describe a small shop that sells fashionable clothing, gifts, or jewelry. The word fashion comes up time and time again in definitions of the boutique, and most specify that a true boutique must be small.

For the purposes of this book, we define a boutique as a small retail store, usually less than 2000 square feet, and often closer to 1000. The main product a boutique sells is generally used for adornment, such as clothing, accessories or shoes. Secondary products could include cosmetics or other items that complement a fashionable look.

The popularity of the boutique is partly due to the fact that many consumers prefer shopping for products or services on a cozy and intimate scale. The department store with its vast square footage, multiple levels, crowded elevators and slow escalators can seem like a real time-drain.

As a side note, the term "boutique" is also now used to define select small hotels, ad agencies, investor firms, etc. that offer personalized, attentive service. The term has been borrowed by non-retail industries to convey the close, cozy feeling that an intimate retail experience has to offer.

A boutique can sell its products to women, men, children, teenagers, or all of the above. Its focus might be large people, small people, vintage souls, glamour girls or lovers of denim. Your imagination is your only limit. We'll discuss later in this guide how to find a niche for yourself in the boutique market.

Since so many boutique owners pursue a fashionable flavor, let's define fashion, too. In a general sense, fashion is a way or manner of doing something. It's the current custom followed by a defined group of people. Specifically, fashion refers to the latest trends in clothing, shoes and accessories, and the business of designing, manufacturing and selling the same.

Don't confuse fashion with clothing. There are large sections of the clothing market that have little to do with fashion. Not all of what we call fashion means clothing, and not all clothing is fashion. However, be aware that there is a lot of overlap.

Fashion is a fun business and a fickle one. You'll probably have noticed that on the most scorching days of late July, wool sweaters and coats start to arrive in many shops. By September, just as the weather is cooling, many of these things are already on sale. That's the nature of the fashion cycle.

Fashion is hot when it's new, and it can get cold almost as fast as a plate of spaghetti. If your niche is very classic cashmere sweaters, tweed skirts and strings of pearls, your product will be less perishable than the trendy styles that grace the magazine covers.

While clothing rarely rots or grows mold, it is vulnerable to the passing of time, just as the apples and tomatoes at your local greengrocer are. Its shelf life may be longer, but it's just as important to move the goods while they're fresh.

# 1.2 The Boutique Owner

Not too many people open up new department stores these days (unless they've won big in the lottery or wound up with an unexpected inheritance), but lots of people open their own boutiques. Some of these people start small, but many eventually expand to a cluster of small shops, or to a store that grows to take up twice the square footage it did on opening day. Two of the people interviewed for this book now own several boutique locations, and almost all have expanded beyond their original store size.

To help you tap in to what it's like to own a boutique, we'll share opinions and insider tips throughout the book from the boutique owners we interviewed. Let's introduce you to them now.

- Sue joined forces with three partners in 1992 to purchase four already-established but failing boutiques. Today Sue owns seven boutiques called Tall Etc. that specialize in fashions for the tall woman.

- Beth and Jacquie turned a love of yoga into a successful business retailing yoga clothing and accessories. They manufacture some of their own products, import others, and offer website sales to expand the client base of their small shop.

- Beverly owns a consignment shop specializing in vintage fashion. She and her partner started business with a cash injection of only a few hundred dollars, and then Beverly bought out her partner five years into the business. The business has paid all her living expenses and has broken even for six years running. Now, in its seventh year, it is showing a profit.

- Margaret imports beautiful, one-of-a-kind pieces from Poland and sells them in a touristy, seaside fishing village. Her investment was minimal and she didn't have to borrow anything from the bank. She also managed to turn a profit in her first year of operations.

- Jane wanted to make and sell truly distinctive, high-quality children's clothing. She learned not only how to retail, but also how to design, manufacture and import everything from swimsuits to parkas for children. She now has stores in New York and LA in addition to Seattle, where the business started.

- Wendy began to sew her own designs and recycle her mother's clothes at a tender age. She decided to open a boutique to sell her own creations and included the work of other local designers as well. Twelve years later she still loves her work and her business, and can't imagine doing anything else.

You'll hear from these seven successful entrepreneurs throughout this guidebook, offering their opinions and advice on a variety of topics.

Every boutique will be different because every business is subtly different, and each owner has their own specific background, strengths and weaknesses. Your story will not be exactly like that of anyone interviewed for this book. The exciting thing about opening a new business is discovering exactly what your success story will be.

# 1.3  Benefits of the Career

If you have a love for fashion and the buying and selling of clothing, you are likely to find fulfillment in running your own boutique. Here are some of the benefits you'll experience in this fabulous and exciting career.

## Being a Fashion Insider

Opening a newly arrived box of product can feel quite a bit like Christmas morning. You'll be the first one to slip on and model the latest trends in your community. You'll be surrounded by the work of designers you admire. You'll be among the first to view the newest collections just as they are launched. Your job will require insight as you learn to recognize trends and spot styles that your customers will snap up with delight six months down the road.

You probably enjoy dressing fashionably yourself, and will get pleasure from modeling your own product every day at work. Of course, if your store specializes in underwear or swimwear we'll encourage you to support the other boutiques in your neighborhood to keep yourself covered up... just make sure they know where to find your shop, too!

Your business might require that you travel to New York, LA, or even Paris or Milan to buy product for your boutique. This kind of travel will be a justified business expense and an allowable tax deduction.

## Meeting and Helping People

You'll get tremendous satisfaction from helping someone find an out-fit that suits her figure and coloring, or to choose a gift for someone else. You'll be able to put a reluctant shopper at ease and make him so comfortable in your environment that he'll swear undying loyalty for the rest of his shopping days. You'll feel good about the fact that you helped someone improve their self-image by treating themselves to a flattering, esteem-building new outfit from your store.

On a good day you'll be surrounded by people for hours at a time, usu-ally one or two co-workers as well as a flow of customers from different walks of life. You'll meet new people every day — people from your own retail neighborhood, and visitors from all over the world with varying tastes, interesting stories, and unusual requests. Your regular customers will soon feel like friends.

## Being Creative

This can be a creative job with a lot of room for freedom of expression. You'll be able to try new things with buying, merchandizing and dis-playing the line. Window dressing can be quite a high art and you'll be mingling with other creative people like designers and merchandisers, as well as fashion writers and stylists who come in to find out about your shop.

Your visual flare will extend to putting separates together to make stun-ning outfits and accessorizing them to give them that extra "wow." You'll become handy with a few straight pins as you recommend al-terations to make a jacket or dress look as though it was tailor-made for your client.

## Being Your Own Boss

You'll love making your first big sale and ringing it into the cash regis-ter. You'll enjoy that happy look on your customer's face as they walk out with a new purchase. When customers come in for the first time and express admiration for your boutique and its line of merchandise, you'll feel a sense of pride and accomplishment. At the end of a busy Saturday during the holiday season you will probably even enjoy that bone-tired feeling that comes from being run off your feet all day, because you'll have been working hard to build the success of your own business.

When you start a new business you are by default committing yourself to a lot of hard work. But if you're the type that tries hard at everything you do, then it makes sense to pursue something you love. If fashion is your passion, opening a boutique makes more sense than starting a dry-cleaning business or your own catering company, right?

## Unlimited Income Potential

Retail fashion isn't likely to go away soon. Even though Internet and catalog shopping has impacted the way consumers shop, most people still like to buy on impulse. They like to try clothing on before they purchase it and like to handle fabrics to see how they feel.

Specific buying habits and trends will fluctuate wildly, and the amount people will spend will vary with economic conditions. However, human nature is such that there will always be a market for retail fashion and for general clothing. The challenge is to know the market, study your customers, observe trends and stay ahead of the game.

As the owner of your own business, your income is in your own hands. You won't have to ask your boss to give you a raise; you'll have to figure out how to sell more product at the kind of profit margin that will let you earn the money you want to. Successful boutique owners make a decent living; boutique owners who open multiple locations can make $100,000 a year or more.

We wouldn't say that retail fashion is an easy way to get rich, but there are many examples of people who have built big businesses from very humble beginnings. When you do what you love and do it to the best of your abilities, the money will follow and more importantly, you'll create a life that you enjoy.

## 1.4  In This Guide

As with any business venture, the more research and planning you can do in advance, the better. This book will assist you by getting you to ask and answer the questions that should be resolved before you decide to take that big step. We'll also make sure that you have as many practical tools as possible to ensure the viability of your business.

Chapter 2 (*"The Boutique Environment"*) introduces you to the world of the boutique, with a look at retailing fashion, what the marketplace is like for boutiques, what the owner of a boutique will do from day to day, and how you can develop the skills you'll need to succeed.

Chapter 3 (*"Planning Your Boutique"*) really gets your creative juices flowing. You'll learn how to get inspired, how to hone in on a niche market, and what your business options are. Then you'll see how to pull it all together into a viable business plan, how to calculate your start-up costs, and find out how to shop your plan around to lenders and investors.

Chapter 4 (*"Preparing to Open"*) gives you detailed and thoughtful advice on how to select the location that will give you the best chance of success, where to find suppliers locally, nationally and internationally, how much inventory to start with, what mix of product to buy, and it explains how boutiques set their prices. The chapter concludes with tips on hiring great staff members (even if it's only one or two) and the business details you'll need to take care of before you open, from licenses to insurance.

Chapter 5 (*"Running Your Boutique"*) offers a practical guide to operating your shop once it is open for business. It covers key operational issues like merchandizing, effective sales techniques, day-to-day operations from cash handling to theft prevention, and managing your staff. This chapter also shares expert advice on attracting customers to your boutique through conventional and unconventional ways. Finally, it concludes with a look at the ins-and outs of one of the hottest trends in boutique retailing these days: the bridal boutique.

Chapter 6 rounds out the guidebook with a list of additional resources, publications, associations and websites to help you on your path to learn even more about boutique ownership.

And throughout the guide you'll find bits of wisdom and advice from successful boutique owners who were kind enough to share their experiences with you, the reader. So if you're ready, let's get started!

# 2.  The Boutique Environment

The boutique environment is varied, flexible and often fascinating. After you've read this chapter, step into a boutique and look at the garments on the racks. You'll probably look at them quite differently. You might look beyond the finished garment itself to think about not only its designer, but the fabric's designer and the color forecasters responsible for that precise shade of plum.

You'll think about the sales agent or distributor who expressed an interest in selling the line, and about the buyer who decided that this pleated silk skirt would be a good item to sell in the specific shop where you now stand. You'll consider the dozens of people involved in the process from the initial concept to the final finished article.

## 2.1  Retailing Fashion

To retail merchandise is to sell it to the general public. Anyone can walk into a retail store and buy something as long as they have the money or credit to pay for it. This differs from wholesaling, which is the term for selling goods in larger quantities and at lower prices to retailers themselves, not directly to the public. A shop can retail anything from bicycles to bikinis, stereos to Stilton, but if you walk through any major retail neighborhood you'll probably find that fashionable clothing dominates the market.

## 2.1.1   A Historical Perspective

The concept of retailing fashion is quite recent. In the 19th century, people either bought fabric and sewed their own clothes, or they bought fabric and paid dressmakers to sew for them, depending on their social class. Although those dressmakers were technically fashion designers, they were nothing like the demi-gods of today. For this we can thank Charles Frederick Worth, Paul Poiret and finally, the woman who truly changed fashion for all of us, Coco Chanel. Her influence is legendary and her story makes for fascinating reading, especially because of her rise from poverty to the world-famous fashion icon that she later became.

Chanel dared to introduce menswear styling for women. She did two of the things that we're going to stress throughout this guide: she understood her market, and she offered them something unique that they couldn't find anywhere else. Chanel is also significant to the boutique world because she retailed her own designs, and what began as her small hat shop evolved into what could be considered fashion's first boutique. Women who came to Chanel for hats openly admired her own liberated, comfortable sense of style. Soon they were asking her to make them versions of her shorter skirts and loose-fitting shirts, styles that they couldn't find from any of their usual dressmakers.

Chanel of course obliged, and soon her line included the famous pearls, shoes, handbags and perfume. As her popularity and the demand for Chanel-style grew, obviously she could no longer custom-make clothing for all of her customers, so she began to mass-produce her fashions in ready-to-wear styles and sizes.

Chanel inspired designers all over Europe and North America. You can read about Chanel and the other original fashionistas at About.com's Women's Fashion: Famous Fashion Designers Throughout History at **http://fashion.about.com/od/famousdesigners**.

## 2.1.2 Why We Buy Clothing

Let's face it: if clothing today had not significantly evolved from the animal skins that our cave-dwelling ancestors pulled on for warmth, the retail business would be a tiny fraction of what it actually is. Those first garments were simply to protect us from the elements. Clothing today still does that. It gives us warmth and protection from wind, rain, and sun exposure. It also covers nakedness to ensure modesty. However, these functions are almost incidental in the scope of the fashion business.

If clothing was primarily for warmth, the color wouldn't matter, nor would the cut or silhouette. We would be happy to slip into a wool jacket, but we wouldn't go into ecstasy over it. Fashionable clothing is not about protection from the elements or modesty. It expresses identity, and our belonging to a specific group. It makes us attractive to the opposite sex as well as to our peers, potential employers and business associates. It suggests a level of affluence that means we can afford the latest designer trends.

Fashion is to people as packaging is to product and as book covers are to the text inside them. It's how we sell ourselves, how we express both our individuality and our willingness to conform to a certain code. It's also how we feel good about ourselves.

One reason why fashion is one of the easier product ranges to sell is the ever-changing desires of a group called the fashionistas. These are the designers, color theorists and trend forecasters at the top of the style hierarchy. These creative geniuses kick-start each season by deciding what is hot, current and desirable in attire. They may decide one year that brown is the new black, or that cobalt blue is suddenly a neutral, thereby banishing last year's clothing to the box of Goodwill donations. Because of the fashionistas, hemlines are thigh-high one spring and reaching the ankle by fall.

It is the ever-changing nature of fashion that persuades many women, almost all teenagers, and a growing proportion of men to replace a significant chunk of their wardrobe each season. That's what feeds the fashion cycle. That's what turns shopping into a quest for the perfect new look. That's what makes it fun, and that's what brings consumers into clothing boutiques, day in and day out.

## Who's Who in Retail Fashion

The fashion cycle is kicked off by the designer, who comes up with an initial overall concept for a line or a collection, as well as the look of the individual pieces. Normally she will decide on the fabrics and colors to be used and make a sketch that the pattern-maker then uses to create the pattern and the first sample.

Manufacturers are often large organizations that employ a designer or many designers, sometimes to produce a number of different collections or even a series of brands. A manufacturer might also have purchased the rights (licenses) to manufacture the products of a select high-profile designer.

Distributors usually represent a foreign designer or manufacturer. Their role is similar to a sales agency, but they don't normally collect a percentage of the selling price as payment. Instead, they agree to a special unit price from the manufacturer and mark up this merchandise to the wholesale customer (you). They also would normally physically distribute the product rather than just take orders for it.

As a boutique owner, your vendors or suppliers in most cases will be designers, manufacturers, or distributors, although most of the time your buying will be done through a sales agent. Agents are self-employed and they usually have one or more showrooms, and often represent one or more designers.

The buyer is the person who views the designer's or manufacturer's samples and writes the purchase order for the merchandise to be delivered to each store. She needs not only a sense of what her market will like, but how much of it a given store will require, in what colors and what size mix. She's also responsible for checking delivery dates and negotiating payment terms. When you own a boutique, the buyer is most likely you.

## 2.1.3   The Fashion Cycle

One cold day in February you might cheer yourself by going into a store for a look at new spring clothing. So you roam the shop, looking at the colors, prints and style details. You may pull a blouse off the rack and handle the fabric.

What you may not realize is that the actual creative process it took to make that item probably started 12 to 18 months ago. The designer was probably looking at a sample piece of that same fabric in January or February of last year. The amount of time involved can vary, but generally the more fashionable and high-end the label is, the longer the process will take from conception to "in-store date."

### The Process

The trend forecasters and color stylists would have put their savvy heads together with the designers at the fabric mills to create a seasonal palette. They examine a range of social, market and economic factors to decide whether tropical colors will be hot, or pastels, or earth tones.

Some designers might have already started making their first sketches and will have a fabric in mind for a given garment. Others will only become inspired as they see and touch the new fabrics. Then they'll start on the patterns and will begin sewing the first samples.

It will take from about 3 to 6 months for them to get every design detail just right, from the cut of the garment to buttons, zippers and trims.

Then they produce the selling samples that buyers look at, and from which they place their bulk orders. From there it can take up to another six months for the manufacturer to order and receive production fabrics; and then cut, sew, package and ship all of the garments ordered by customers.

## A Sample Cycle

Let's look at a sample garment design and production cycle to get products into stores for Spring 2010:

| | |
|---|---|
| *Fall 2008:* | Color forecasting and fabric designing begin. |
| *Winter 2008:* | Fabric is shown at trade shows; designers order fabric. |
| *Spring 2009:* | Designers work on first patterns and samples. |
| *Summer 2009:* | Samples manufactured and shipped to sales reps. |
| *Fall 2009:* | Buyers view samples and place garment orders. |
| *Winter 2009:* | Ordered garments are manufactured. |
| *Spring 2010:* | Orders are shipped to retailers. |

This is an example only; every production cycle will vary. Still, you now see how long the process can take.

This helps you to understand that if you run out of a certain celery-colored blouse in size 8 on a Thursday, the supplier might not be in a position to ship your replacement stock so that you have it in store for the following Monday. If you're lucky they might have a small amount of inventory available for re-orders, but if not, it is unlikely that they will be able to make more within a reasonable time frame.

## Fashion Seasons

Traditionally, fashion's seasons have been broken down into collections of appropriate weight clothing for spring, summer, fall and winter. They lined up as follows:

| | |
|---|---|
| *Spring:* | Light twill trousers, blouses and raincoats |
| *Summer:* | Sundresses, halter tops, shorts and bikinis |
| *Fall:* | Back-to-school items, corduroy pants, sweaters, long-sleeved shirts and blouses and medium-weight jackets |
| *Winter:* | Similar to fall, with heavy coats and fancy dresses |

Deciding this was not enough to meet the buyers' needs, many designers added a separate season for:

| | |
|---|---|
| *Holiday:* | Selection of party dresses and skirts, satin trousers, evening bags, etc. for Thanksgiving, Winter Holiday parties and New Year's Eve |
| *Cruise:* | Collection of summer shorts, swimsuits and cabana wear for winter vacations in tropical places |

Typically, Cruise can ship as early as December but is more likely in store in January. Spring ships from early January to late February, with Summer usually in store by the end of March. Fall arrives from early June through August, and Winter is usually complete in September or October, with Holiday close on its heels; it should be in stores well before the U.S. Thanksgiving holiday.

Over the years many manufacturers have moved towards offering mini-seasons so that retailers can receive new product on a bi-weekly or monthly basis. This is an effective way for boutiques to buy, because it's easier to lure the curious customer in to your shop when you have fresh stock arriving on a regular basis, rather than four to six times a year.

## 2.2  The Boutique Marketplace

Retail stores are generally classified as department stores, chain stores or boutiques. Department stores like Barneys, Nordstrom's, Neiman Marcus and The Bay group their product into departments like women's wear, men's wear, children's wear, cosmetics, accessories, house wares and furniture.

A chain is a collection of stores, sometimes operating under different retail names, but owned by the same big company. Individual locations within a given chain would share the same atmosphere and similar merchandise. Think of The Gap as an example, which owns not only The Gap stores, but Banana Republic and Old Navy.

A boutique, as we explained earlier, is a smaller store. Often (but not always) it focuses on one category of product, like women's clothing, men's wear, children's wear, lingerie, shoes or accessories. Boutique product tends to be fashionable rather than just functional and often features one or more designer labels. Sometimes even a small store will decide to carry a selection of women's, men's and children's clothing, but for effective merchandising they will focus on a very few designers, or a specific product like footwear, or a narrow theme, like the active sportswear trend or safari-jungle theme.

The single boutique as a business can grow and become a chain as additional locations are opened. In fact, your boutique might eventually become a family with branch stores in different parts of town, or from coast to coast! Traditionally a boutique was a brick-and-mortar store — a physical location with an address and a front door. These days, a boutique can be different. You can rent a tiny kiosk in a busy mall, and from it run a boutique that sells scarves or hats or jewelry or clothes for dogs. Or you can have a virtual boutique with an online presence only.

## 2.2.1   The Boutique is Chic

You may be intimidated by the thought of competing with mega-stores like The Gap, but the boutique offers strategic advantages. As a small retail machine it is far more efficient than the chain or department store. It's much easier to change course according to fluctuating market conditions — to react in time by purchasing more product or a more expensive product range if the economy suddenly booms.

"I love boutique retailing because you can react fast. The small scale allows you to turn on a dime. You can change the whole direction of the business very quickly if you have to," confirms boutique owner Sue.

A boutique has a number of options to be competitive. Customers might appreciate a certain ambiance you create with lighting, décor and fixtures, music and mood. It might be in a neighborhood that makes it convenient. Courteous, professional service is also a basic requirement. And of course, while these things are important, it will be the merchandise itself that keeps a customer coming back on a regular basis.

## Making a Profit

Your boutique might be a pleasant place to hang out for five or six days each week. It might be more fun than an office job. However, ultimately to be successful your boutique is going to have to make you a profit.

When the merchandise is paid for, and the rent, utilities, staff wages and your own salary are all paid, the boutique should have something left in the bank. It shouldn't drain your resources indefinitely, and it shouldn't just break even.

As we said, the fashion product is perishable in the sense that if it doesn't sell within the peak season, chances are it will have to be discounted, cutting heavily into your profit margin. The goal of any retailer is to sell the product as quickly as possible, before the competition is reducing everything by 20% and more. But of course if the product sells too fast and you haven't planned for fresh inventory, you'll have an empty store. It's a fine balance that all boutique owners have to work on developing.

Naturally, profitability doesn't happen over night. It takes time to build customers' awareness of your shop and develop a steady clientele. We'll take a detailed look at profitability and what you can reasonably expect later in this guidebook.

## The "Fabulous Four"

This guide is going to stress four very important points throughout that are key to the success of your boutique, which we'll call the "fabulous four." We'll introduce them right up front here, and come back to them often.

### #1: Business Mentor

Find a mentor, ask him or her questions, and listen carefully to that advice. That doesn't mean necessarily following every suggestion, but listen to what they say and evaluate it thoroughly. The mentor should have experience in owning a boutique or at least a small retail store.

### #2: Location

Give significant thought to your location, the surrounding retail neighborhood, and how strong your market is in that area. Don't let emotions guide you into signing a lease on a boutique that you love, but that happens to be in a failing shopping district. Don't agree to a place that is twice the space you need or can afford.

### #3: Niche

Consider your niche: the specific type of product you plan to offer, the size of the market demanding such a product, and growth prospects for that niche. Your niche (area of specialization) and location are your two most important decisions. Both deserve a lot of thought.

### #4: Finance

Make sure you're realistic about the financing you require, and the amount of capital you'll need to start the business. One of the most common reasons for failure in any kind of business is being under-financed.

## 2.2.2  Common Myths

We'll bet you've already come across a few of those nay-sayers. You know, the ones who act like you're crazy to even consider starting your own business. They might have told you stories about the people they know who've started their businesses and failed miserably.

Well, we'd like the gloomsters to meet Sue and Janice and Margaret and the countless other entrepreneurs who have started their own boutiques and made them thrive. We'd like to talk to those people who didn't make it and find out how many of them had mentors, and how much time they spent doing research.

But probably no success story would change the pessimistic mind. Nor would it matter if you were suggesting something highly practical, like becoming a dental hygienist or starting a bookkeeping business. The truth is that the nay-sayers don't really want you to succeed. They don't want you to fail, either. They just don't want you to do anything different. They're afraid of change, be it yours or theirs.

Here are a few of the other myths about opening and running a boutique you might encounter along the way, and reasons why you shouldn't let them sway you from your dream.

## Myth #1:  You need to look like a runway model to sell fashion.

It helps to look good in clothes and enjoy wearing them, but it's actually more effective to resemble the average customer who will be walking through your doors. If a customer sees you looking great despite being short or carrying a few extra pounds, he might be more likely to think, "Maybe that guy could put together an outfit that would suit me too!"

And of course you can be any size and shape to sell children's clothing, or shoes or accessories. An outgoing attitude and a friendly disposition will take you to success much faster than a fashionable figure will.

## Myth #2:  A small boutique will never make a lot of money.

It's rare for a boutique to turn a fat profit quickly, but some of the boutique owners interviewed for this book turned a profit in their first year of business. More often, slow and steady wins the race. With careful financial management and reinvestment of the first profits, a boutique can grow into a larger store or a family of shops in various locations that can make a significant profit.

## Myth #3:  You need sales experience to sell effectively.

Sales experience seldom hurts your business, but you don't want to come off as a professional closer, someone who pushes and won't take no for an answer. That kind of shop gets a reputation quickly, and often the customers are terrified to walk through the door, no matter how inviting your windows are.

You should come across as a person first, rather than a salesperson. A natural enthusiasm for your product and a genuine desire to help people look their best will get you much farther than a high-pressure approach. We'll give you some tips on developing a natural sales technique later in this guide.

### Myth #4: Retailing fashion is a crowded market where only a few survive.

Fashion can be competitive. Any kind of retail can, but competition isn't all bad. It tends to bring out the best in us and make us try harder. As we've stressed throughout, it's possible to position your business in such a way that the competition is incidental. Come up with a unique concept that will put you in a category with a strong market but minimal competition.

### Myth #5: You need to be super-wealthy to open a boutique.

If only the super-wealthy ever opened boutiques, there would be hardly anywhere for the rest of us to shop. It's true that you need a certain amount of start-up capital, but there are ways to keep your budget relatively lean.

Unless you open a small consignment store on a skinny budget, chances are the funds required to make it a success will be more than you have sitting in your piggy bank. But most people who start up businesses don't do it exclusively with their own money. We'll look at financing options as well in this guide.

And finally, maybe you've come across one or two people who say, "A boutique? Lucky you! That'll be an easy business to run." Well, they're wrong, too. There will be days when it is hard work. Even the fun parts, like the buying, will seem like hard work at times. But hard work is gratifying, especially when you're working for yourself.

## 2.3  The Owner's Role

You already know about the perks of opening your own boutique: Buying trips! A great wardrobe! Working with fashion! Interacting with people! Being rewarded for your own business savvy and creative ideas! And you love fashion. If you want nothing more than to immerse yourself in that world, read on.

As the owner of your boutique, your job will extend well beyond selling a product to clients. The owner of a boutique is responsible for everything from its initial design and merchandise concept to making sure the bathroom is clean and taking out the trash. You'll also be responsible for:

- Attending fashion shows and show marts to scope out new product

- Staying abreast of trends in fashion and in retail concepts

- Purchasing merchandise to sell

- Receiving shipments

- Designing or overseeing the merchandising of your products

- Setting the prices

- Monitoring sales and financial performance

- Long-term budgeting

- Paying bills and making deposits

- Monitoring inventory and placing orders

- Hiring and managing staff

- Handling client complaints

- Marketing and promoting the boutique

## 2.3.1  Hats You'll Wear

Naturally you might decide to hire employees to assist with many of the tasks, but at first you should at least be prepared to do a lot of the work yourself. You should also be familiar with every aspect of the job so that you can train your staff to do things exactly the way you want them done.

Margaret knew nothing about computers when she bought one to track her orders, sales and inventory, but she chose to enter all the data by herself, step by step. By inputting all the information, she felt confident that if the system ever went wrong, she would be able to sort out the error herself. If she had paid someone else to program the data she would have had to call them every time she had a problem.

"If you want to run your own business you can't pay other people to do all the work. You have to know your own business from the bottom up. No job should be too low," agrees Sue. Here's a more detailed breakdown of some of the hats you'll need to wear as a boutique owner.

## Merchandiser/Window Dresser

You will be in charge of deciding how to display product, what fashion mood to promote and how to most attractively exhibit the mix of merchandise on hand. On the first bright spring day you might decide to move all the tropical colors to the front of the store and keep the blacks and neutrals at the back. In January when you have little new stock and you're trying to promote the end-of-season sales, you'll want to make sure that the racks at the front of the store all have "Sale" signs that draw customers in.

Although some boutique owners choose to hire window consultants who will visit the shop every week or two, in the beginning you might reduce expenses by doing your own windows, especially if you have an artistic flair and you enjoy the work. There are lots of helpful books on the topic, but your best education will be looking at the striking windows of other boutiques you admire.

## Garment Buyer

Most boutique owners buy the merchandise for their stores by themselves. If the business grows substantially you might hire an assistant buyer or ask your store managers for input, but this is one of the parts of the job that most owners like to keep hands-on. You have to put yourself in the heads and hearts of your customers. You'll also develop a sense of what sizes are going to sell, and in what mix.

## Sales Consultant

Sales drive the success of your business and put profit into your pocket. As the owner of the boutique, you'll set the selling tone of your shop. You'll learn to increase your sales by suggesting the perfect belt or necklace to go with an outfit. You'll also be able to suggest what shoes and accessories might dress an outfit up or down, and how a client might get more mileage from an expensive blazer.

# A Typical Day

How do you know that the job of owning a boutique is for you? What is a typical day like? Imagine a Friday morning like this…

The shop has just opened and things are quiet as your retail neighborhood begins to wake up. You've got a coffee tucked discreetly behind the sales counter and your favorite mellow CD is on the stereo.

A customer walks in through your front door. You recognize her from a few months back. That time she needed a few pieces to take on holiday with her and a dress that she could wear to a wedding in the south of France. Today she's wearing one of the outfits from your store and she looks fabulous.

She comes up and tells you how perfect the pieces were for her vacation and how simple they made packing her suitcase. She received countless compliments at the wedding and she's been telling all her friends about your shop.

She wants to see what's new, and you show her the latest collection from your favorite up-and-coming designer. You just finished unpacking it the day before. She buys a new sweater and goes back to the office to show it off. You've made your first sale of the day!

More importantly you've been appreciated for the product and service you offer. You're full of a warm, fuzzy feeling that has little to do with the cha-ching of the cash register. You've helped make someone look good and feel good about her image and get more from her vacation. She's so thrilled with your shop that she's telling the world, promoting your business in a way that costs you nothing more than thoughtful service and a warm smile.

Later in the day you might receive a new shipment of more clothing. You'll have to count it, unpack it and probably steam it before hanging it up in your store. You'll have to prepare a bank deposit at some point, and will probably write a few checks to pay the bills. You'll indulge yourself in a fashion magazine with lunch or coffee; part of your job is to stay on top of what's hot.

Later you might want to feature some of the new stock in the window and change the displays throughout the store. Or you might need to re-merchandise the shop so that the exciting new product is evident as soon as your customers step through the front door. Then at the end of the day you'll count the cash, lock up, and go home to rest up for another busy day!

The best boutique staff members are adept at dressing their customers, instinctively knowing what colors, textures and cuts of clothing will flatter them, and recommending them in a way that is never pushy. As the leader of your staff, you'll be a winning consultant yourself, and it will show with every customer you assist. This personal service sets the high-quality boutique apart from the run-of-the-mill establishment.

## Super Service Expert

Customer service means being prepared to bend over backwards for a good customer, like offering to get a patient husband a latte from the café next door while he sits and waits for his wife to try on a half-dozen outfits. It could mean personally bringing a few items to a visiting client's hotel room one evening if her schedule doesn't allow time to visit your store during business hours.

It also includes knowing how to be diplomatic when a customer has a real or imagined grievance, and keeping detailed customer records about past purchases so you can call to let them know about new arrivals and special promotions.

## Public Relations and Marketing Specialist

You will be responsible for coming up with creative and affordable ways to spread the word about your boutique, both leading up to your grand opening, and on an ongoing basis once you are up and running. You may create some of your ads or copy yourself, or you might assign a graphic artist or ad agency to come up with something fun and funky to turn heads. Either way, the last word on how to promote your boutique will be yours.

## Human Resources Manager

You'll be responsible for recruiting, hiring, scheduling, evaluating and promoting staff. Should you choose to hire a manager they can take over some of this role, but it will be in your best interest to stay involved to an extent.

You'll also need to train each new person you hire, not only with practical details like using the computer and cash register, but on daily procedures like cleaning the store before it opens each morning. Your staff will be the first face of the boutique that potential customers encounter, so you want to know that face well, and what it communicates about your boutique.

## Bookkeeper

You'll probably contract the accounting out to a professional unless you're a qualified accountant, but you might choose to learn enough basic bookkeeping to take care of the daily entries. You'll have a better understanding of your boutique's cash flow if you look after the basics, and well-kept books mean that the fees you have to pay an accountant will be lower.

## Occasional Roles

These roles aren't necessarily a regular or even common part of your job, but situations might arise requiring you to act as:

- *Shipper/Receiver:* Not the most glamorous part of the job to be sure, but there might be days when you're the only person working in the store when a shipment of new stock arrives. In some cases you may ship items out to clients who can't make it into your store, or who place an order online.

- *Computer/Cash Register Technician:* You should know your computer system and cash register better than anyone else, so that you can correct simple errors, look up inventory, and generate reports that tell you what last month's top-selling style was.

- *Therapist:* People can't help bringing their personal lives to work sometimes. If one of your staff is noticeably upset because she's broken up with her boyfriend, you'll want to take her into the back room with a box of tissues and a sympathetic attitude.

- *Referee:* If your staff is on a bonus or commission structure, you might have two employees in dispute over who approached a customer first or something similar. In this case you'll have to hear them out and decide how to resolve the problem.

- *Janitor:* Your boutique should be spotless at all times. Your staff should help you by maintaining a tidy boutique and staff room, but when you start small, a lot of the dusting, polishing and vacuuming will be up to you.

- *Security Force:* There's a chance you'll catch someone trying to shoplift or make a purchase using a fraudulent credit card. You'll need to contact the police and file a report when they arrive.

## 2.3.2 Traits of a Successful Owner

No two boutique owners are going to be exactly alike, but if you talk to a few of them, most will share several of the characteristics listed on the next page. Think about whether these are qualities you already have, or areas that you could develop with a bit of time:

- Self-direction

- Fashion and color sense

- Independent thinking

- Good listening/interpersonal skills

- Financial discipline

- A positive attitude

Let's look at each of these skills one at a time, and consider what you can do to strengthen your abilities if they aren't already top-notch.

# Self-Direction

You won't be an employee when you have your own boutique. No one will tell you what to do and when or how to do it. You'll have to motivate yourself and learn self-direction. If this doesn't come naturally to you, a bit of practice will make it easier. Self-direction and self-discipline are habits that can be acquired in less time than you think. And of course motivating yourself to do the things that need to be done in your boutique will be easier when there's a financial "carrot" dangling at the end of the stick.

Start with small things. Force yourself to get up five minutes earlier each day, then fifteen, then half an hour. When you have an extra half-hour, use it to focus your mind. Consider a morning meditation or just sit quietly and plan your day.

Make a list of goals for each day, each week, and each month. Monitor your progress. When you reach a goal, reward yourself with a small but meaningful treat. If you miss a goal, don't beat yourself up about it, but consider why you didn't make it. Think about what steps you could have taken, or what you could have done differently.

# Fashion and Color Sense

Study fashion magazines and fashion TV. Don't just observe passively, but really get involved. Why does that outfit work? What makes it look good? Or maybe it doesn't work, and you don't like it.

Read designer interviews and bios. What makes them tick? What inspires them? Can you see the average customer embracing that new look, or could you adapt it in some way that keeps it fashionable but makes it more practical? What can you do to update your own wardrobe and look more stylish without spending a lot on new fashions? How do accessories work to change the look of an outfit?

Don't just dwell on your favorite colors, but think about the entire palette and a range of hues or intensities. What colors work together? What feels quietly pleasant and peaceful? What combinations feel exciting or dynamic? Can you find examples that break the rules and combine unlikely colors in effective designs? What makes it work? When doesn't it work?

# Independent Thinking

Being fashionable doesn't mean being a sheep. Develop your own style. Reject new things for your own wardrobe if you don't like them, but don't automatically reject them for your boutique if they seem popular with large numbers of potential customers.

Be independent with your taste in films and music too. So it won an award and everyone's talking about it. Why? Is it really good? Does it have true merit, true quality? Think for yourself. You might choose not to express every individual idea, but it's to your advantage to have them.

# Good Listening/Interpersonal Skills

Remember that the Golden Rule is to treat others as you'd like to be treated yourself. Treat all customers as you like to be treated when you're a customer, but probably rarely are.

"One thing that's worked in my favor is that I seem to have a great memory for names. I remember what they bought the last time they came in. That helps me understand their tastes. I can give them better service by showing them the things they're most likely to love right away," Beverly told us.

Practice listening to people without interrupting. Wait your turn. This is much, much harder than you might think. It might surprise you to learn how tempted you are to butt in with your own opinions or your own version of events. Listen and attend to the speaker. Don't let your mind race ahead with its own ideas of what you will say when you have the chance, just listen.

# Financial Discipline

If you're trying to set money aside to invest in your boutique, this is an excellent time to practice the financial discipline you'll need when you're running your own business. Develop a personal budget and try to stick to it. Monitor how much you actually spend each day, each week, each month, and try to track it by category (e.g. rent/mortgage, groceries, eating out, entertainment, clothes, etc.). Again, if you stick to it, reward yourself. If you go over in a category, just think about why.

Maybe the budget was unreasonable, or maybe you made an impulsive decision.

## A Positive Attitude

There is no substitute for a healthy attitude and the personal conviction that you can make your boutique a success. All the start-up capital in the world can't bring customers into your door if there's a gloomy dark cloud of "I can't" hanging over the front entrance. If your boutique bubbles over with positive energy and an upbeat mood, people are going to be attracted to it like nails to a magnet. They'll notice a certain new buzz of excitement in the neighborhood air, and they'll just about *have to* pop their heads inside for a peek.

So believe in yourself and in your boutique. Nothing happens first without being imagined. No business ever got off the ground by accident. Now it's time to reprogram your thinking, to repeat a daily mantra of "my boutique is a success." In fact, those amazing people who write books on positive mental attitudes always say that your affirmations should be stated as if in the present, as if the thing you want is already true.

If you need to boost your self-belief you should consider reading some of the books that encourage a positive mental attitude. There are several excellent ones on the market; here are a few that might make a good start:

- *The Magic of Thinking Big,*
  by David L. Schwartz

- *Follow Your Heart,*
  by Andrew Matthews

- *Born to Succeed,*
  by Colin Turner

## Other Important or Helpful Qualities

- Ambition

- Motivation

- Honesty/fairness/integrity
- Organizational skills
- Enthusiasm
- Sense of humor
- Outgoing disposition
- Curiosity
- Interest in trends and designers
- Leadership skills
- Good research and analytical abilities
- Creativity
- Imagination
- Intuition
- Eye for the aesthetic
- Natural sales ability
- Charisma

And finally, one quality that is not necessary but it sure won't hurt: a generous inheritance!

## 2.3.3   Quiz: Are You Ready?

Now you know a bit more about the reality of running a boutique and the nature of the fashion industry. How do you measure up? Are you ready for the challenges, the busy days and the hectic, bustling environment? And don't forget the buying trips — days of excitement where you must be on your toes and ready to make sharp business decisions for hours on end.

Take the following quiz to evaluate your own qualities and how they might assist you in running a successful boutique.

# Self-Evaluation Quiz

Decide how strongly you feel about the following statements, and circle your response on a scale of 1 *(Strongly Disagree)* to 5 *(Strongly Agree)*.

| | Strongly Disagree | | Neutral | | Strongly Agree |
|---|---|---|---|---|---|
| 1. I love fashion and I always keep abreast of the latest trends. | 1 | 2 | 3 | 4 | 5 |
| 2. I prefer a classic, timeless look and do not follow fads. | 1 | 2 | 3 | 4 | 5 |
| 3. I am familiar with the top designers and the look identified with each. | 1 | 2 | 3 | 4 | 5 |
| 4. I understand a bit about fabrics and quality workmanship. | 1 | 2 | 3 | 4 | 5 |
| 5. I have worked in a retail environment before. | 1 | 2 | 3 | 4 | 5 |
| 6. I have sold clothing, shoes or accessories in the past. | 1 | 2 | 3 | 4 | 5 |
| 7. I am patient. | 1 | 2 | 3 | 4 | 5 |
| 8. I have worked with the public either in person or on the telephone. | 1 | 2 | 3 | 4 | 5 |
| 9. I am sociable and love working with people. | 1 | 2 | 3 | 4 | 5 |
| 10. I have a good visual aesthetic sense. | 1 | 2 | 3 | 4 | 5 |
| 11. I am comfortable contacting strangers by telephone. | 1 | 2 | 3 | 4 | 5 |
| 12. I am financially disciplined and am able to stick to a budget. | 1 | 2 | 3 | 4 | 5 |
| 13. I like working with numbers. | 1 | 2 | 3 | 4 | 5 |
| 14. I enjoy helping people look and feel their best. | 1 | 2 | 3 | 4 | 5 |
| 15. I like to travel and spend time in large cities. | 1 | 2 | 3 | 4 | 5 |
| 16. I am organized and I keep good records. | 1 | 2 | 3 | 4 | 5 |
| 17. I am diplomatic and have good leadership skills. | 1 | 2 | 3 | 4 | 5 |
| 18. I am good at making decisions. | 1 | 2 | 3 | 4 | 5 |

To evaluate, take a look at where the majority of your answers fell. You might be ready to go out and get started right this minute, or you might decide that doing some extra reading or gaining a bit of experience is the best thing to do while you work on your plan.

Don't be concerned if you scored a number of 3s and a few 1s. Neutral or negative answers don't mean that you couldn't run a successful boutique. For example, many of us aren't very disciplined about budgeting in our personal lives, but we do learn to stick to the plan when it involves the higher stakes of a business. And many of us wouldn't normally consider ourselves extroverted, but we find that we quite enjoy talking to people about something that we love, like fashion!

Even when it comes to understanding math and formulas, a problem about two trains approaching each other at different speeds might make our eyes roll, but understanding the profit on a blouse that cost $20 and sells for $55 is a piece of cake. Consider the nature of these questions, and decide whether you could benefit from brushing up on certain skills, as explained in the next section.

# 2.4   Ways to Learn More

We're willing to bet that you already have a lot of what it takes to run a successful boutique. If an area of expertise falls outside of your skill set, there are a number of ways to increase your confidence. This section is devoted to helping you acquire the knowledge and skills that will make you a success.

## 2.4.1   Find a Mentor

Before you open your boutique, part of your research should involve talking to people who already own successful boutiques. If you can get these people to talk shop with you candidly, the information will be more relevant than anything you can get from a paid training course. This type of relationship is called mentoring, and usually does not involve any exchange of money (like a consultant would charge) but is simply one business person helping another out.

This kind of chat with another store owner will probably divulge some of the same kind of helpful advice we got from boutique owners for this book. The difference is that you'll be getting details specific for your region and/or your market niche, which a book cannot do.

## Who to Contact

We suggest that you approach boutique owners who will never be in direct competition with you. That means choosing at least one or two boutique owners who run the style of boutique you are interested in, but are in other towns. The further away the better, so make sure you're on the lookout the next time you go on vacation or spend a weekend out of town.

You can also interview one or two business owners who are already set up in the area you want to be in, but who have different kinds of shops. Talk to the toy store owner, the florist, or the manager of the fitness club. They can help advise you on the nuances of the area. There should be things that you admire about this shop, other than the fact that it is well established and apparently successful.

If you can't find a mentor among your family, acquaintances, and friends of friends, consider contacting SCORE (**www.score.org**), the Service Corps of Retired Executives, which is an association with chapters in many major cities.

These brilliant volunteers have run all kinds of businesses and are now donating their time to answering questions from people just like you. You can get free advice online, or you can arrange to meet someone in person at one of their regional offices. If you're lucky you might get assigned to someone with retail experience, but even if they've come from a different field you're likely to get solid, valuable advice.

## How to Approach

There are a couple of ways to go about approaching a store owner. You could just wander in and look around as if you were a customer. In fact, it certainly wouldn't hurt to make a small purchase from the person who might be in a position to give you some valuable tips.

We strongly recommend choosing a day when the shop is likely to be quiet, so you aren't taking their time away from paying customers. You might break the ice by making a sincere compliment to the person working in the store. Maybe you like their windows, or their stock, or the store design.

Be chatty. How long has the store been there? How has business been in the last few months? Ask if he or she is the owner. If so, you could explain that you also intend to open a boutique back in Other Town, or a non-competing boutique in the same area. Explain that you'd love to buy them a coffee or lunch if they have a few minutes to talk to you about the business.

If the person you've been speaking to isn't the owner but is the manager or a full-time salesperson, they are still worth talking to. They probably won't have answers to all the questions you want to ask, but they'll know a lot about walk-by traffic and sales. With luck they'll give you a business card for the owner and you can call her or him later.

Few people will refuse you outright. They might be too busy to have coffee with you, but could invite you to stay and chat with them as long as you understand that the customers will come first. Alternately you could ask if it's okay to phone them one evening. But as long as you're friendly, grateful and non-threatening, chances are they'll talk to you about their business.

## What to Ask

If you develop a close relationship with a mentor there are few things you won't be able to ask them, but at first they probably won't want to divulge personal or financial information, like how much they spent starting their business, what kind of salary they've been taking or how much profit they're making.

However, they might be willing to tell you how they go about sourcing their product or forecasting trends. They might tell you what trade publications they faithfully read, what local contractor they hired to look after their store build out, what computer system seems to work for managing their sales reports and inventory — that sort of thing.

They might tell you when their busiest day of the week is and what months have historically been the best for sales. If you're lucky they'll share details like how the weather tends to affect customer traffic and how business has been on statutory holidays. They could tell you the best way to advertise for staff and give you a few hiring tips.

If you strike up a real rapport with the person, you can ask them if they would be willing to be your actual "mentor". Make it clear that you would never take advantage or ask them to lend you money. You just want someone who'll be there to ask questions of from time to time, someone to give you advice now and then as you take your first steps. Assure them that if they'll give you a lunch hour occasionally you'll treat them to the sandwiches, and that you'll always be respectful of their time.

Here are some suggestions for general questions to ask boutique owners, but obviously you should feel free to develop your own list according to the questions that are burning to be answered. Try to ask open-ended questions that will elicit more than a simple yes or no. You want to get these people to really talk to you!

---

## Mentor Questionnaire

In what ways has the reality of running a boutique been different from what you imagined?

_____

_____

_____

Is there any one pearl of wisdom you can share with me, something you've learned along the way that you wish you'd known when you started?

_____

_____

_____

What has been your greatest, most memorable moment as the owner of this boutique?

_____

_____

_____

---

Are there any disappointments, letdowns or problems you've encountered that you can share?

_____

_____

_____

What relevant experience did you have when you started out?

_____

_____

_____

Did you have a mentor? If so, in what ways have they helped?

_____

_____

_____

Did you buy an existing business or grow it from the ground up?

_____

_____

_____

If you could wind back the clock and start over, is there anything you'd do differently?

_____

_____

_____

What has been your biggest surprise, the one thing you didn't see coming?

_____

_____

_____

Have you expanded from the original store, or have you immediate plans to grow the business?

_____

_____

_____

## Taking it with a Grain of Salt

Boutique owners Jacqueline and Beth want to stress the importance of filtering the advice you'll get and only following the best of it. An overwhelming, opinionated mentor could do your business (and your ego) a fair bit of harm. "A mentor needs to understand what your business is like and not tell you what to do, but rather ask you questions that will lead you to making sound decisions on your own," advises Beth.

You'll need to distinguish between a real mentor and a person who just has opinions. Find some support, but find the right kind of support. Don't follow bad advice.

How to know the advice is bad? If your gut feeling tells you that you don't agree, listen to that instinct. And always consider the source. Someone with 20 years' experience retailing men's shoes isn't necessarily the person to advise you on how to buy product for your lingerie store.

## 2.4.2   Formal Education

Whether or not you need formal education and training is usually dependent on your previous experience in fashion and retail, and your current educational background. The most relevant education to this career would likely be fashion merchandizing or business/entrepreneurial courses, although just about any background from fine arts to accounting would give you a leg up.

Some, but not all of the boutique owners interviewed for this book had college-level training in fashion merchandising or business. A few had university degrees in the arts, but virtually no retail business experience.

Margaret attended a local fashion merchandising college, and later worked as a department head in a nationwide department store. The latter gave her experience with buying, which proved invaluable, but she was quick to point out that you don't need both retail experience and schooling to succeed. "School and real life are completely different," she confesses, and the work experience has probably contributed more to her success than the textbooks did.

If you'd feel better with some relevant education behind you, there is the option of fashion merchandising programs to consider, and the option of training from home. For example, Ashworth University offers an online Fashion Retailing program at **www.ashworthuniversity.edu/ programs/business/fm/**.

Many colleges and universities offer excellent continuing education courses on a variety of business topics as well. These are condensed programs available during evenings and weekends. You can brush up on your bookkeeping, study business writing, or learn about image consultation.

Many major cities also have relevant programs through the local technical schools, with courses offered in evenings or on weekends. Some of these will relate to fashion and you might be able to learn fashion merchandising or the basics of design, image consulting, window displays, etc. There's a listing of general fashion arts programs at **www. FashionSchools.com**. In Canada, you can find schools offering fashion programs at the School Finder website (**www.schoolfinder.com**), by typing "fashion" into the "Program Search" on the main page.

## 2.4.3   Work in a Boutique

We can't over-emphasize the importance of having some boutique-specific retail experience before you strike out on your own. You don't need to spend a lot of time working for someone else. You might want to work part-time over Christmas, or one evening a week during the summer months. Even a little current exposure to the retail world will prepare you for your new career as a business owner.

> **TIP:**   If you have experience in retail but it was a number of years ago, remember that technology has changed a lot. Most cash registers are run by computer now, and you'll see payment by debit cards a lot more often than checks these days.

If you are not in a position to go work in a shop for little pay, though, it's not the end of the world. "If you're savvy and you start up within a small community where you have strong relationships, you might be able to open a shop with no previous retail experience and still do quite well," advises Sue.

# How to Get Hired

Rewrite your resume with a focus on anything fashion-related and any kind of retail experience. If you've volunteered to help coordinate a charity fashion show, make sure you put that in. Express an interest in fashion. Experience working with customers will help too.

Resumes don't have to be chronological anymore; you're allowed to summarize your work experience according to the kinds of jobs you've done and the skills you've acquired. In fact, many employers appreciate that because it makes it easier for them to find what they're looking for.

Leave resumes at all the boutiques and department stores you can think of. Don't wait for advertised job postings, just drop off resumes in person when you're smartly dressed, and mention that you're looking for part-time work. Often it's your image, your demeanor and your attitude that will get you the job. Store managers and boutique owners can have a difficult time finding and keeping good staff, and finding someone who's willing to work part time can be even more of a challenge.

In the interview, you don't want to mention that you are planning on opening up your own boutique in a few months, or chances are you won't get hired. They might appreciate your initiative, but most employers want to hire someone who's going to be around for a while.

If you're a tiny bit bothered by the idea of being less than upfront with your employer, remember that your enthusiasm to learn all about the business will probably make you the best part-timer they've ever had!

# Making the Most of It

While you are working there, imagine the boutique as if it were your own. Maybe you'd do the displays differently, or have a more customer-friendly exchange policy. Maybe you'd choose to play jazzier music on the stereo, or use a different kind of shopping bag. Immersing yourself in this environment will help you answer questions about your own boutique.

It will also help you ask the questions that you wouldn't otherwise have thought of, and "test out" everything from software programs to alarm systems. Maybe the store has a few bugs or awkward operations. Aren't you better off finding out on the system that someone else has paid for?

Finally, remember that when you're on the employer's clock, you're looking after their business, not yours. It would be a little bit tacky and a lot of bad karma to slip customers your business cards, or to tell them to come and see you next week at your new boutique.

# 3. Planning Your Boutique

The key to success in any business is to do a good amount of initial research, and to use your instincts. Few people actually enjoy digging up details on demographics and market potential, but that groundwork becomes a lot more fun and significant when you know it's going to contribute to your success. It's to your great advantage to learn as much as you can before you start the business, rather than six months into it.

So let's do the research before you sign your lease or a single purchase order. Let's do things right from the beginning and think it out step by step. That's what this book is all about. We'll walk you through the process and help you with the decisions you'll face at each step of the way.

## 3.1 Get Inspired

*"If you've got a dream, go for it. Follow your passion, even if it seems scary and people tell you it's impractical. Life is too short to do work that you don't love."*

— Beverly, Boutique Owner

At this point, in your mind's eye you may have a vision for your boutique. You might see paint colors on the walls or the view of the storefront from the street. Maybe you can see the sequins on a selection of formal gowns, or satin slippers with rhinestones and beaded handbags displayed in your shop.

Remember that first you have to imagine something before it can become real. Now is the time to brainstorm ideas, and get them all down on paper. Here are some ways to get inspired with ideas for your boutique.

## 3.1.1   Study Other Boutiques

You probably already have a few favorite haunts. These are places you like to shop partly because of the merchandise selection, but also because they are comfortable places to be. Something about their ambiance attracts you.

If you're like most people you won't be able to pinpoint exactly why they make you feel this way. You know you like them, but the specific qualities that attract you remain elusive or undefined. Well, it's time to start thinking critically by looking at them differently.

Make several copies of the questionnaire you'll find in this section, and take them with you each time go shopping from now on. Rate each business according to the questions listed. Later, fill out the comments section and provide as much detail as you can for any element that stood out as being particularly good or bad.

> **TIP:**   You don't have to limit your research to clothing boutiques — music shops, book dealers, stationers and even cafés can provide you with insight (although some of the questions are specific to clothing).

In addition to visiting boutiques in your area, Visual References Publications (**www.visualreference.com**) can be an excellent source of inspiration. They publish books and magazines with photos of unique and inspired retail design.

# Boutique Questionnaire

## Accessibility

Did you walk or drive?

_____

_____

How was parking?

_____

_____

How does the neighborhood feel – is it safe?

_____

_____

Would you feel comfortable at night?

_____

_____

Is the street free of garbage and panhandlers?

_____

_____

## Outside Appearance

How does the boutique look as you approach it?

_____

_____

Is the front entrance tidy and inviting?

_____

_____

Is the name on the sign legible?

_____

_____

Does it identify the type of business?

_____

_____

Are the windows attention-getting?

_____

_____

Do they reflect the mood of the shop?

_____

_____

Is the glass clean?

_____

_____

Is the exterior paint fresh or shabby?

_____

_____

Do you like the color?

_____

_____

## Inside Look and Feel

How is the décor/theme/color story of the store?

_____

_____

Is it well laid-out?

_____

_____

Is the lighting attractive and effective?

_____

_____

Are interior displays well put together?

_____

_____

Are the colors/patterns/styles of the materials in stock well merchandised and attractively grouped?

_____

_____

Is it easy to find what you're looking for?

_____

_____

Is it tidy?

_____

_____

Is it open and airy, or claustrophobic and crowded with too much stuff?

_____

_____

Is there a noticeable scent in the air?

_____

_____

If so is it pleasant and clean, or musty?

_____

_____

Are there food aromas from nearby restaurants?

_____

_____

Music: how is its mood and volume level?

_____

_____

Is it the sort of sound you'd like to hear in your own boutique?

_____

_____

**The Staff**

Did anyone acknowledge you?

_____

_____

Were they friendly?

_____

_____

Did they offer to help in a pushy way, or just pleasant?

_____

_____

Did you feel judged by the way you were dressed?

_____

_____

Were they cordial and attentive, or busy talking amongst themselves?

_____

_____

If you asked questions, were they knowledgeable about the product?

_____

_____

**Merchandise**

Was there much to interest you?

_____

_____

How were the styles?

_____

_____

How were the colors?

_____

_____

How was the size range?

_____

_____

How was the overall selection?

_____

_____

Was there a good assortment of tops/bottoms/jackets/etc.?

_____

_____

Was it easy to find your size?

_____

_____

Was there a logical system, or did the staff assist you?

_____

_____

**Fitting Rooms**

Were they clean?

_____

_____

Did the curtain or door give you enough privacy?

_____

_____

Was there a chair or a hook for your coat or handbag?

_____

_____

Was there a full-length mirror inside the fitting room?

_____

_____

Were there enough rooms, or did you have to wait?

_____

_____

**Purchase and Exit**

Was it easy to pay for your purchases?

_____

_____

Did you have to wait?

_____

_____

Did the staff know how to use the computer?

_____

_____

Was the payment policy convenient?

_____

_____

What is the exchange/refund policy?

_____

_____

Did they wrap your purchase in tissue before putting it in a bag?

_____

_____

Do you like the style of shopping bag?

_____

_____

Did the staff mention how to care for your purchase?

_____

_____

Did they thank you for coming in and say goodbye?

_____

_____

Were you left with the feeling that you wanted to come back?

_____

_____

**Other Comments**

_____

_____

_____

_____

_____

_____

_____

## 3.1.2 Brainstorming Exercises

It's time to start dreaming about your boutique, in vivid, Technicolor detail. Get it all down and remember that this is no time to be hesitant. Dream your boutique and dream it big.

Remember, it's your boutique and your dream. Open yourself fully to creativity and allow yourself to include even your wildest imagining. You must give your ideas a home, a place to gestate, and some room to start believing in themselves.

## Start a Boutique Journal

Start a journal and write down everything you can think of about your boutique. Don't be practical in your boutique dream journal; there will be plenty of opportunity to be practical later. This is your creative brainstorm. Make the most of your ideas.

- Make a sketch of a display that inspires you, or enter the name of an unusual or new designer you discover in someone else's store or in a magazine.

- Start a list of the CDs you want played in your boutique and brainstorm any innovative promotional ideas.

- If you're starting to consider different names for your boutique, devote a page to your journal where you jot down every name that comes into your head.

Cut pictures out of magazines, not just of clothing, shoes and accessories, but of interior design aspects, such as:

- A fabulous counter with a glass display inset for accessories

- A wonderful antique mannequin

- A "just-right" armchair

- A chip of paint for the wall behind the cash desk

- A swatch of fabric for the fitting room curtains

- An elegant bit of script that you might be able to use in your logo or signage

- A business card for someone who says they do custom cabinetry and shelving

## Consider Mood and Theme

Use the images in your journal to focus on your boutique's intended mood, ambiance or theme. Do you see something slick and modern with a lot of glass and chrome? Or something warmer, with Victorian dressers used to display product, area rugs and the old-fashioned dress-form type of mannequin? Maybe your theme will be Asian with a lacquered screen in one corner and a Buddha guarding the cash desk, potted bamboo and polished wood floors.

Ambiance is a special atmosphere or mood, which is created by a particular environment. While it might seem like a term reserved for a spa or restaurant, it applies to retail spaces as well. It could mean the difference between a customer entering your boutique or walking by, and may also determine the length of their stay.

Trying to achieve the right ambiance for your boutique requires careful consideration of your niche market and appealing to at least three of our senses: sight, hearing and smell.

Sight relates to the overall look of your boutique. Are there wood panel walls creating a sense of rural elegance? Are there posters of pop stars creating a young, hip atmosphere? Is the furniture modern or classic? Is the color scheme calming or vibrant? A big part of creating visual ambiance in your boutique is your lighting — keep in mind the message you convey with how your boutique is lit.

Hearing is, of course, referring to what customers are listening to in your boutique. Try to match the type and volume of music being played in your store with the mood that you're trying to achieve. Beyond music, customers will also overhear your staff's conversations, so a rule that keeps certain topics or offensive words in the staffroom should apply.

We all know the power that smell has on us — think about how a restaurant or coffee shop lures people into their establishment with fresh aromas of food and beverage. While smell may not have the same impact with your boutique, it can still play a role. Fresh flowers, potpourri and various commercial scents can help create an ambience that defines your boutique from the rest.

You might even decide to keep a minimalist look with concrete floors and exposed beams and no clutter at all. In this case you'll want the interior displays to be striking and attention-getting. Just remember, there's a fine line between spare and cold.

The ambiance you intend to create should ideally reflect your product and should definitely put your customer at ease. You don't want a lot of breakable lamps, vases or glass tables in a children's wear store. In fact, for children's shops, you'll probably want to go with a brighter color scheme and possibly a corner with a few toys to occupy small kids while mom takes her time looking at your merchandise. The Victorian theme might not make a whole lot of sense if you're selling designer athletic wear, but it could be perfect for lingerie or classic menswear. The "Zen thing" might be perfect for a line of yoga clothing.

Ask yourself to imagine your average customer in the environment you create and make sure you settle on something that will make them feel at home. Then try to work all the other elements around the overall theme.

## Bare Essentials and Lovable Extras

The "bare essentials" is where you'll list your absolute minimum boutique requirements. These are things you and your boutique cannot live without — the things that are so important to you that without them, you'd rather just not play the game. This could be anything from the entire Moby collection on CD, to chocolate-colored velvet curtains for the fitting rooms, to a skylight or a small fountain.

It's okay to be inflexible about a few things. After all, this is your baby, your dream. You're putting heart and soul into it and you deserve to create the store you want. Just don't let this list get too long. Otherwise you'll never settle on an appropriate space, or you'll find it difficult to stick to your start-up budget.

Make a photocopy of the bare essentials list and use it to keep you on track when looking at spaces. As you walk through any location, imagine your essentials, where they would go, how they might fit in. This way it will be easier to look at a location and see its potential to feel like your own.

The "lovable extras" list is different from the one above. These are things you can live without, if you have to, but if they're affordable and possible to include they would add something great to your boutique — the kind of "wow factor" that will make customers want to come back time and time again.

This is creative brainstorming where your wish list can be unlimited. You're just getting down ideas that will set a distinct, personal stamp on your boutique. Exposed brick walls? A wicker divan? Circular cash desk? Get it all down, but don't let yourself become attached to any of it just yet.

## 3.1.3 Choosing a Name

Earlier in this section we asked you to start listing any possible names for your boutique that came into your head. Eventually you will be whittling the list down until there are a few that stand out as likely candidates. What do you want from a name? Here are a few things to consider:

- It will have to be available. You'll register the name as your own, a name that your boutique can legally do business as. Therefore you can't take a business name that someone else already owns, like Macy's or The Limited, or that is very similar to an existing name.

- If you plan to have a website, you should also choose a name that has a domain name available, ideally ending in the most popular '.com'. A company like GoDaddy (**www.godaddy.com**) allows you to search for and register available domain names.

- It should be memorable, not too challenging to pronounce and not too complicated to spell. If someone drives past your window after store hours and falls in love with the coat displayed, you'll want them to be able to look up the name of the shop in the morning and call to ask you about its availability.

- It should suit the product and the overall concept of your shop. You probably wouldn't choose to call a children's wear store Rock Chick Fashions, or a plus-size shop Twiggy's.

Many boutiques are named after their owner's given name or surname. Presumably it works for many of the entrepreneurs who have gone that route, but they aren't always memorable unless the name is easy to spell and pronounce. The signage should be legible and the name should show up clearly on your stationery, business cards and packaging.

Consider the name's relationship to the overall brand identity and corporate image. If your surname is Butt, you might be tempted to display some family pride by calling your shop Butt's. However, whatever your given or surname is, think twice before you give it to your business as well.

- What are the connotations of your name?

- Is it distinctive?

- How about positive?

- Is it automatically associated with something desirable?

- Does it suggest a lifestyle or a product that your customers will instinctively crave?

Here are a few boutique names already in use that stand out in a way that's especially memorable, and are effective at promoting the concept of the shop. They might inspire your train of thought!

- *Fab:* Trendy/designer young women's fashions, high-end

- *Barefoot Contessa:* Feminine young women's clothing, slightly European in theme

- *Bratz:* Designer children's wear

- *Karma:* Yoga clothing and lifestyles

- *Boy's Company:* Young men's designer fashions, high-end

- *Bodacious:* Plus-sized women's secondhand fashions

- *Secondhand Rose:* Vintage consignment fashions

- *Chocolates for Breakfast:* Elegant, upscale women's attire

- *Lil'putians:* Children's wear

You can learn more about finding a name for your business at Nolo. com's Business Resources website at **www.nolo.com**. Click on the "Business & Human Resources" tab, then on "Starting a Business," then on "Naming Your Business".

Marcia Yudkin, a marketing specialist, has a helpful (and free!) 19-step guide online at her website for choosing a business name and tag line, which you can access at **www.yudkin.com/generate.htm**.

## 3.1.4   Logos and Branding

There was a time when starting a small business meant little more than finding the right location, the right product, the right price and offering your customer the best possible service.

Those things are all vital to a successful business, as we've stressed throughout the book. But in the contemporary marketplace there are other things to consider as well. These fall under the subject of branding. A logo for your boutique is essential, but there's a bit more to the aspect of corporate identity, which we'll explain below.

### Your Logo

You're going to need a logo that is a distinctive corporate emblem and a way of presenting your business name on signage, bags and boxes, business cards and stationery. This is an important detail and it's worth consulting a professional graphic designer to get an attractive, distinctive logo that says exactly what you want it to about your boutique and its products. This is probably not one of those things you should try to do yourself unless you have a strong design background. Designing logos is a very specific talent and a professional logo will give your boutique that stamp of quality.

Graphic designers are plentiful, so chances are that you already know someone who knows someone. Work with the designer to choose a font or lettering style that expresses the individual character of your boutique and then include any other symbols or illustrations that you think are relevant.

If you don't know a graphic designer, a very affordable solution is the LogoSmartz software package. You can design your own logo from one of their templates, or create your own using industry-specific graphics. You can view a demo at their website, as well as download a demo copy at **www.logosmartz.com** to try it out. Cost for the software is $39.95.

Copyright the logo so no one else can use it. Then have it printed over and over again anytime you need new cards, shopping bags, envelopes or gift boxes.

## Branding and Corporate Identity

Your brand is more than just your trademark; it's the web of associations that customers will connect with your business. It's a promise of exceptional quality, or personalized service, hip style selection or competitive pricing. (Note that rarely does it promise all of these!) Your brand is the character of your boutique.

A strong brand identity makes customers feel as if they "know" the personalities behind the business and it contributes to customer loyalty. It will keep customers coming back to your shop because they will feel convinced that your shop is "their" shop and you are likely to have the things they want to buy.

Is it essential to actively brand your boutique? Not necessarily, especially if you buy designer labels that already have a strong brand identity. However, if your competition down the street or across town carries those same labels, and they have managed to create a brand that appeals to a huge section of your market, many of your customers will take their business to that store and their brand.

Branding is not essential to every business, but it has become essential to creating an identifiable product that stands out in the minds of consumers. There are a lot of boutiques out there with little or no brand identity, but the truly successful shops will have created a brand through a solid consistency in name, logo, store design, product and staff.

Brand is intangible, but it is not accidental. The most successful corporations hire very savvy brand managers or consultants to help them create, or re-create a brand. Branding is what makes consumers perceive Volvo as different from Volkswagen. It's what inspires people to willingly label themselves as Pepsi or Coke drinkers.

When your brand filters through to every aspect of your business, including the store design, the product range, the music and packaging, you will become a leader in your field. Customers will find themselves returning to your boutique because they enjoy the experience and the feeling of belonging. They'll make a habit of visiting your store to check out fresh stock every week or two.

This is a difficult concept to express, but it's fairly simple to illustrate. Think about The Gap. Visualize its signage, store appearance, the type of product they carry and the typical salesperson. The corporate image is youthful, casual, and pretty wholesome, right? You'd probably be surprised to see someone obviously in their fifties working at The Gap.

Imagine their logo, the simple capital letters on the navy background. You probably wouldn't expect to find lacy underwear in the store, or a business suit, or a floor-length silk taffeta skirt. But it might be the place you automatically think of when you're in the market for chinos and button-down shirts.

Now think of other stores, and try to visualize their corporate picture in the same way. Think of how DKNY, Guess or American Eagle Outfitters feel different from The Gap, even though their market may have some crossover. Now think about a different kind of clothing, like Anne Taylor, Armani or Chanel. Naturally their product range is more high-end, but brand goes beyond product. You'd probably be surprised to find the same type of shopping bag or lighting, or the same employee working at both kinds of stores.

There's an interesting article you can read online about the importance of branding, using FCUK (French Connection UK) as a case study. You can find the article at **www.buildingbrands.com/didyou know/20_fcuk_fashion.php**.

If your budget permits it and you aspire to grow an empire, it's probably worth consulting a branding specialist before you design your logo or choose a name. Look under "Marketing Specialists" in your Yellow Pages, or do an Internet search for branding companies in your area.

## 3.2  Your Niche Market

Unless you already have a specific niche in mind, it's time to focus on the kind of products you'll carry. You may love all fashion, but there are many sub-sections within the clothing market.

Are we talking the latest in designer women's wear? Sporty casual threads, or the high glamour of the evening dress? Tailored suits for the power executive? Do you want to carry nothing but the best, most exclusive selection? Or do you want to have a bit of fun and try to keep everything in your shop under $40 retail?

A boutique's niche doesn't have to be defined by a specific product category; it can be an overall mood or theme, like romance, or surf and skateboard style, or a store where everything from pants and jackets, skirts and dresses are offered only in denim. Think about what niche you want to satisfy, who will buy your fashions, and what you will offer that the competition does not.

# 3.2.1   Specialties to Consider

If you haven't settled on a niche, you can think about each of these in turn and where you might see a market for your boutique. For convenience we've grouped different categories under the loose headings of women's, men's and children's, though of course your boutique could serve all these markets with a specialty product instead, such as a family shoe store.

Within each category there's definitely room for you to further define your niche. For example you could choose to open a bridal boutique that specialized in vintage looks from the '50s or '60s, or you could import crocheted bikinis from Brazil. Just remember to evaluate each idea according to the size of the market likely to support it. Section 3.2.5 will help you focus in on what it means to be truly unique in what you offer.

## Women's Wear

Women's wear is a good bet for a solid market, because so many women enjoy shopping. It's a social activity, and entertaining in a way that, perplexingly, it rarely is to men. When women discover a shop they love, they tell their girlfriends. When women get poor service at a shop, they also tell their girlfriends.

Many women are fickle about clothing, too. Sometimes they absolutely must have a new pair of jeans, even when there are no fewer than six in the closet. Maybe the pockets or topstitching will be different, the leg a little more flared, or the denim a slightly lighter or darker shade. Ditto for the tailored white blouse, the black turtleneck, the sheath dress — one is rarely enough.

It's easy to narrow your focus within women's wear and decide whether you want to buy junior, trendy lines, or feature something more elegant. And of course when you decide on the style itself you can further carve your niche:

- Accessories

- Beach/swimwear

- Bridal

- Business/career attire

- Casual wear/jeans

- Formals/eveningwear

- Hats

- Hosiery

- Junior/teen

- Lingerie/sleepwear

- Maternity

- Outerwear

- Shoes

- Special sizes: petites, plus, tall

- Sportswear

- Sweaters

- Yoga or active wear

Many successful clothing boutiques have started carrying a small selection of shoes intended to coordinate with the style of clothing they sell. It's a good option if you don't want to focus on shoes exclusively.

Fashion trends in women's shoes fluctuate as wildly as the cut of jeans or the hemline of skirts, so women need to update their shoe selection frequently to be in style. Selling bridal wear is also a popular niche right now, and you can read all about how to sell to and serve this specialty market in section 5.6 of this guide.

## Men's Wear

Traditionally men do not "love" shopping, although statistics suggest this is changing in urban markets. An emerging trend called "manity," a term coined by futurist Faith Popcorn, suggested that men would show a sharply increased awareness in matters of beauty and grooming. Now beginning to manifest itself, you'll find many men go to hair-stylists instead of barbers, visit spas, have manicures and occasionally get waxed.

It makes sense that fashion follows. You can count on a decent percentage of urban males to buy very trendy designer clothes. They might just spend a few hours on a weekend combing boutiques to see what there is to offer. This appears to be good news for the men's wear boutique owner, but remember this trend is most evident in urban centers.

The smaller towns of North America still teem with the "old-school" male for whom shopping rates somewhere between a doctor's appointment and a tax audit. Most of them buy clothes because they have to — there are holes in their old chinos and their shirts are threadbare at the elbows. They won't buy clothes simply because the old ones are out of style. The fact is, they won't always know that the old ones are even out of style. So remember, you're up against a customer who doesn't necessarily want to be there.

However, even in the smallest town you won't just be selling to the reluctant male. You might be carrying clothes ultimately intended for the male body, but women are often the buyers of their husbands' and boyfriends' clothing.

Because there's a large market for men's business clothing, many men's shops carry only suits, dress shirts and ties. It is less common to see a shop specializing in men's underwear than women's lingerie, but in a city of a certain size there might be a market for such a small, specific store.

Most often a men's boutique will carry a selection of a few different types of products, like casual shirts and khakis with a few coats and a selection of socks, which allows men to get their shopping done in one stop. Think about:

- Business suits

- Casual wear/jeans/khakis

- Formalwear

- Outerwear

- Shoes

- Socks

- Special size: tall, big, short

- Sportswear

- Ties

- Underwear

- Watches

## Children's Wear

Children's wear can be a strong market, because children grow so quickly and are so active that they require new clothes each year. Also, retailers have found that during an economic slowdown, parents will spend money on their children's clothing before they buy for themselves.

With younger children the ultimate selection decision may be the parent's, but normally the child's tastes are taken into account. And children's tastes can be surprisingly well-developed from a tender age. Pre-adolescent children often have their own money to spend on clothing, sometimes without their parent's direct involvement, although it is often understood that the purchase must meet with mom or dad's approval. If the parent vetoes the turquoise fun-fur jacket, back to the shop it will go.

Most children's stores will carry a wide variety of products, and may include numerous accessories as well. Children's shoes are often sold separately, but usually underwear and sleepwear are offered within a larger, more general kind of store. Depending on the market, though, a tiny store offering just children's pajamas and nightgowns could still do well. Consider:

- Infant clothing

- Bedding and accessories

- Formal/party clothes

- Shoes

- Swimwear

- Used/consignment items

## 3.2.2   What Customers Want

To answer the question of what customers look for in a boutique, you're going to have to think long and hard about who your customer is. It would be much simpler if all customers wanted the same thing, but nothing could be further from the truth.

## Different Strokes for Different Folks

Not all customers want hot pink tube tops or grey pleated skirts — that's a given. The tougher concept to grasp is that not all customers want the same retail experience. Not all want the lowest price available, and not all want what you and I might consider exceptional service. Not all customers even want quality, and those who do prioritize quality may define it differently. It's a subjective concept.

For example, the female teenager who watches MTV and pores over consumer magazines will insist on up-to-the minute fashion.

- A garment's overall trendiness and the fact that it looks good on her will weigh far more heavily than the concept of whether the fabric is of good quality and whether the workmanship is up to scratch. Chances are the garment is only intended to last a year or two anyway, until it is out of style.

- For this customer, a low price point will be an advantage. Unless she's got a good job or a healthy allowance she won't have a lot to spend on her wardrobe, and she will be motivated by sales.

- Good service will mean a comfortable environment where she likes the music. The staff will make her feel welcome without pressuring her into anything. They'll chat in a friendly way and will be happy to help her find other sizes, or suggest different ways of coordinating her outfit.

In contrast, the middle-aged woman who favors tweed skirts, cardigans, pearls and sensible shoes doesn't have much interest in fashion.

- She does insist on quality and she'll define it as well-made fabrics from primarily natural fibers, appropriate linings, buttons securely sewn and a recognized but not whimsical label that she can count on.

- She won't necessarily be a bargain shopper, but she certainly won't want to feel she's been taken advantage of.

- Good service will mean a courteous greeting but not necessarily a chatty conversation about her weekend. It will mean the opportunity to return anything she's not happy with, having the door held for her when she leaves your shop, and your attempt to special order something she likes but hasn't been able to find in her size.

The business executive, socialite and working mother will also have their own expectations from your shop. Observe your market. Visit the kind of shop you aspire to have and watch "your" customer enter the boutique. Try to absorb the experience through their eyes. Make notes as to what you think is effective, and what you think might be lacking.

## The Female Client

Women buy almost everything. Of course they buy women's clothing, shoes and accessories. Mothers also buy clothing, shoes and accessories for their kids, and wives, girlfriends and sisters buy for the men in their lives, and for other women.

Women shop for themselves more often than men do. Their wardrobes and shoe collections are generally more extensive and they update them more frequently. Walk through any shopping center. We'll bet you find at least two women's boutiques for every menswear shop. Their business attire requires more flexibility and they change more of their wardrobe with each season. Fashions in women's clothing also change more radically each season than men's do.

Even in a shop that sells to both sexes, there will usually be more area devoted to women's wear. Department stores usually have at least a floor and a half of women's wear to every floor of men's wear. Think of the intimate apparel section alone: men's underwear may be getting more stylish, but there's still a much broader selection and demand for women's lingerie. Women also buy a greater range of accessories such as scarves, handbags, costume jewelry and hair ornaments.

## The Male Client

Men quite often buy their own wardrobe, and very occasionally buy clothing for women, but not nearly as often as women buy for men. Of course there are exceptions, and men in larger urban centers are more

likely to be comfortable in women's boutiques shopping for the women in their lives.

Quality men's clothing often costs a bit more than similar items for women, so they might spend more on any given purchase, but that still won't likely result in the overall sales volume that a woman's purchases would. However, here is an interesting point for those considering a men's wear boutique: because they don't tend to enjoy the process of shopping, some men like to get it all over with at once. If you're a lucky boutique owner, a man might come in and buy four shirts, two pair of trousers, a T-shirt, a jacket, a pair of shorts, sandals and running shoes all in the same afternoon!

A man is also more likely to revisit a boutique where he feels comfortable. If he likes the style of clothing you carry and the service hits the right note, he will be more likely to become a loyal customer than the fickle woman who always wants to go find the next great little shop.

## The Young Client

Toys are marketed directly to children, but clothing is more often marketed with the parent buyer in mind. Children occasionally buy their own clothing, but more often they shop with a parent and with a parent's guidance. Adolescents are more likely to do their own shopping, and many would rather write an algebra exam than be seen in a mall with a parent.

Children's wardrobes need updating often for obvious reasons. They grow out of all kinds of garments. They also play hard in their clothes and get dirty so their things need to be laundered a lot, which shortens the lifespan of a garment.

If you satisfy both a parent shopper and their child, they just might become loyal customers who do all of their back-to-school shopping at your boutique each August. And when the new baby comes along, the amount of purchasing will double.

## 3.2.3    Analyze the Competition

There has long been and always will be a good market for fashionable clothing. Even during World War II there was a black market in Europe for silk stockings. From this perspective it would seem that the only thing standing between you and your extremely successful boutique is the competition.

When you think about it, that fact should be encouraging — you don't have to create a market where one has never existed. All you need to do is satisfy the existing market with a fabulous product selection, the right pricing structure and service beyond their expectations.

The competitive spirit of business should be more like running a marathon or winning a high jump than slaughtering your opponent in battle. There's no need to resort to ugly tactics or downright nastiness with your competition. In a healthy retail climate you can be somewhat friendly with the competition. You can learn from each other, study what they're doing, and then do it that much better.

> **TIP:** Keep your eyes open when you're exploring retail neighborhoods and shopping centers. You might get struck by a part of the market that is not being addressed in your community.

We would never condone directly stealing customers by standing in front of someone else's shop door with a sign that says, "My place has the same Miu Miu dress for $5 less!" We believe in karma, and suspect that most customers are smart enough to detect and dislike any sort of underhanded behavior. Such practices tend to backfire on the people desperate enough to perform them. However, that isn't to say that you can't place an ad in your local paper that reads: "New shipment of Miu Miu dresses just in the door," or "One-day special: 10% off any Miu Miu dress when you buy a pair of shoes." You get the idea.

The competition can work to your advantage too. Let's say your boutique niche is high-end women's separates, featuring designers like Marnie and Prada. Two blocks away is another lovely shop whose niche is high-end women's separates featuring designers like Versace and Escada. Could be trouble, you're thinking? Not necessarily, as long as the neighborhood has a healthy supply of the right kind of traffic.

The other boutique actually helps bring your customer to the neighborhood. They might wander into your store after they visit the competition, and they might not have discovered your shop had they not been there to visit the other one. They might even buy a dress at the competing store, but the coat in your shop on the same day. Or they might keep checking out your product every time they're in the neighborhood and eventually walk out with a new wardrobe put together by none other than yourself.

If you're on good terms with the other shop, a customer will ask them if they carry any Prada. That boutique owner (who you have a friendly relationship with) might say, "We don't, but there's a shop just two blocks up that has a great selection." And of course she'll be more likely to do that for you if she suspects that you'll be happy to do the same. Why not introduce yourself to the competition soon after opening up and start things off on a friendly note?

## 3.2.4   Sell Something You Love

Although it might seem obvious, you should choose to sell something that you love and have a passion for. Perhaps your nickname is Imelda because you have a serious shoe habit. Maybe you've been frustrated by the lack of specialty sizing available and you want to concentrate on petites or plus-sizing, or your passion is to help seniors dress in style. Then again, maybe you drool over darling baby clothes.

But don't open a hat shop if you don't like to wear them. Don't open a children's boutique if the squeal of high-pitched voices gives you a migraine. Don't opt to sell eveningwear if your own personal style is sweatpants. You get the picture. It's much easier to sell something you're genuinely enthusiastic about.

### Interest Questionnaire

If you're having trouble deciding on what sort of boutique category to go for, take the following questionnaire to point you in the right direction. Read each statement and decide where your response falls on the scale. Write the corresponding number in the box at the right of each question.

Then add up your scores grouped by the letter assigned to that question. If you score more than 12 for any category, then that might give you a strong clue as to the kind of boutique environment you'd most enjoy working in. Look at the legend following the quiz for ideas on possible niches that would suit your tastes.

# Interest Questionnaire

Decide how strongly you feel about the following statements, and circle your response on a scale of 1 *(Strongly Disagree)* to 5 *(Strongly Agree).*

| | | Strongly Disagree | | Neutral | | Strongly Agree |
|---|---|---|---|---|---|---|
| 1. | I love using costume jewelry, hats and scarves to create a distinct look. (A) | 1 | 2 | 3 | 4 | 5 |
| 2. | I am a romantic type who loves lace, satin and a feminine look. (L) | 1 | 2 | 3 | 4 | 5 |
| 3. | I watch the Oscars primarily to see what the stars are wearing. (E) | 1 | 2 | 3 | 4 | 5 |
| 4. | I love babies and children. (C) | 1 | 2 | 3 | 4 | 5 |
| 5. | It is hard for me to find clothes that fit me properly due to my size. (S) | 1 | 2 | 3 | 4 | 5 |
| 6. | I am drawn to a specific kind of look, whether it's elegant, ultra-modern, classic or casual. I typically would choose to dress in 4-5 designers exclusively. (W) | 1 | 2 | 3 | 4 | 5 |
| 7. | I am not bothered by noise in my working environment. (C) | 1 | 2 | 3 | 4 | 5 |
| 8. | The perfect vacation is a camping or fishing trip. (M) | 1 | 2 | 3 | 4 | 5 |
| 9. | I have an entire drawer of scarves at home, and a collection of earrings and pins. (A) | 1 | 2 | 3 | 4 | 5 |
| 10. | I am patient. (C) | 1 | 2 | 3 | 4 | 5 |
| 11. | I do not make judgments about others based on their appearance. (S) | 1 | 2 | 3 | 4 | 5 |
| 12. | I like romance novels and old movies. (L) | 1 | 2 | 3 | 4 | 5 |
| 13. | The perfect vacation is a cruise with formal dinners and fancy parties. (E) | 1 | 2 | 3 | 4 | 5 |
| 14. | I get as excited about a new coat as a new pair of shoes or a great-fitting T-shirt. (W) | 1 | 2 | 3 | 4 | 5 |
| 15. | I relate well to men and understand typical male thinking. (M) | 1 | 2 | 3 | 4 | 5 |
| 16. | I am sympathetic to those who are difficult to fit. (S) | 1 | 2 | 3 | 4 | 5 |

| | | | | | |
|---|---|---|---|---|---|
| 17. I love textures and enjoy handling things like wood, feathers and stones. (A) | 1 | 2 | 3 | 4 | 5 |
| 18. I love cocktail parties, weddings and formal affairs. (E) | 1 | 2 | 3 | 4 | 5 |
| 19. I am most comfortable in running shoes, T-shirts and yoga pants. (AS) | 1 | 2 | 3 | 4 | 5 |
| 20. I relate well to women and understand typical female thinking. (W) | 1 | 2 | 3 | 4 | 5 |
| 21. I ski, run, swim or do yoga on a regular basis. (AS) | 1 | 2 | 3 | 4 | 5 |
| 22. I like quiet, muted colors and patterns. (M) | 1 | 2 | 3 | 4 | 5 |
| 23. I understand how to fit a brassiere properly (or would like to learn how). (L) | 1 | 2 | 3 | 4 | 5 |
| 24. The perfect vacation is a resort with endless opportunities for sports. (AS) | 1 | 2 | 3 | 4 | 5 |

## Legend

**C** _____ (score): You like children and maybe have kids yourself. You're patient with children and their parents as they make decisions, and you can help guide them in the right direction. Consider a boutique selling children's clothing and/or shoes.

**A** _____ (score): You love the magic of accessories and understand how scarves and costume jewelry can be used to create different looks. You might want to focus on fashion accessories for men, women or kids.

**W** _____ (score): You're a generalist who is fascinated by women's fashion without leaning toward any particular kind of item. You can narrow your scope by importing a specific look, or by selecting a small range of designers whose styles complement each other.

**AS** _____ (score): You're the sporty type who likes to wear active sportswear on a regular basis and would probably relate well to athletically minded customers. You would find it easy to recommend the right clothing to suit your customer's individual needs.

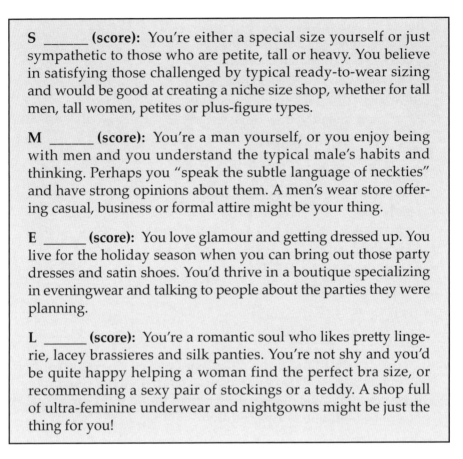

**S** _____ **(score):** You're either a special size yourself or just sympathetic to those who are petite, tall or heavy. You believe in satisfying those challenged by typical ready-to-wear sizing and would be good at creating a niche size shop, whether for tall men, tall women, petites or plus-figure types.

**M** _____ **(score):** You're a man yourself, or you enjoy being with men and you understand the typical male's habits and thinking. Perhaps you "speak the subtle language of neckties" and have strong opinions about them. A men's wear store offering casual, business or formal attire might be your thing.

**E** _____ **(score):** You love glamour and getting dressed up. You live for the holiday season when you can bring out those party dresses and satin shoes. You'd thrive in a boutique specializing in eveningwear and talking to people about the parties they were planning.

**L** _____ **(score):** You're a romantic soul who likes pretty lingerie, lacey brassieres and silk panties. You're not shy and you'd be quite happy helping a woman find the perfect bra size, or recommending a sexy pair of stockings or a teddy. A shop full of ultra-feminine underwear and nightgowns might be just the thing for you!

## 3.2.5   Be Truly Unique

Whatever category you choose to focus on, offer something different in your merchandise, something truly unusual. You want to give people a reason to come to your shop. They won't have that reason if you're carrying a selection that is similar to every other boutique in your category.

You'll also want to think fairly specifically about how broadly you want to define your niche. If it's lingerie, will you include everything from the sexy and frilly to the sportier jersey tanks and briefs? If it's menswear, are you focusing on business attire, casual or both? If you open a shoe store are you going for a conservative career look or the latest trends?

Sometimes it works to combine two niches in one store, as long as you think it will be a convenient way for your market to shop — for example, maternity and infant clothing. And sometimes your boutique will be unique in a way that won't be defined by the niche category; instead it will be reflected in the special product that you offer to customers.

Whatever niche you choose to pursue, make it special. Through your product selection, excellent service and/or fabulous atmosphere, give people a reason to frequent your shop instead of convenient, competitive Wal-Mart.

## Some Real-Life Examples

The vast majority of boutique owners have created a very specific niche to satisfy a market with minimal direct competition. Here's what some of our experts have done.

- Sue provides high-end women's clothing in tall sizes and some plus sizes. The customer base includes professional basketball players and runway models who do not have the option of shopping at stores that limit their product to regular sizing.

- Jane offers a premium-quality line of European-inspired children's clothing with details that are reminiscent of another era. The design is distinctively different from the run-of-the-mill, primary-colored polyester knits favored by major stores.

- Wendy carries local-designer women's wear for a youthful market. The range includes streetwear, casual sportswear, accessories and some lingerie. What makes it distinctive is that 98% of the product is designed and made locally. The store and its merchandise have a unique, distinctive look.

- Beth and Jacqueline sell active sportswear designed specifically for use in yoga practice. Many of the tops, tights and pants can be worn for other kinds of exercise as well, but yoga is the business's reason for being. It has become a huge wellness and fitness trend, and brings a sizeable market to the sportswear industry.

Finally, Margaret's wearable-art merchandise consists mostly of knit linen pieces that are one-of-a-kind, elegant and up-market. She opened her boutique in a fairly low-rent, out-of-the-way, touristy village called Steveston, proving that if you're unique enough, location becomes less important.

Everyone told her not to do it, because there wasn't enough of her high-end market in the immediate neighborhood. They suggested that she open up in an exclusive urban Vancouver neighborhood that would have had lots of her kind of foot traffic.

But Margaret knew that her rent would have been about ten times what it was for the same-sized space in Steveston. She also knew that opening on that scale would have required a bank loan. She was concerned that the pressure of knowing how much she had to sell every day just to pay the rent would have made an uncomfortable environment for both her staff and her customers.

Margaret spent a lot of time watching the traffic move through Steveston. She thought her boutique could do well in the neighborhood. She trusted her instincts and she has grown her business steadily over its first three years. She's been able to successfully break the first rule of location, but only because she went for a truly unique product. "If you want to open a boutique, be unique," advises Margaret.

## 3.3   Business Options

There are three obvious ways to get your boutique started, each with its inherent advantages and disadvantages. The options you'll want to consider are:

- Start a new boutique

- Purchase an existing boutique

- Start a franchise boutique

### 3.3.1   Start a New Boutique

Most of the information in this guide is oriented towards those of you who want to start from scratch with your own business, your own name, your own location and your own distinct product line.

Starting a brand-new boutique, you'll have free creative range and you won't have inherited anyone else's questionable taste or blatant mistakes. You start with a clean slate and everything from the initial niche concept to the name, boutique design and product is up to you.

Of course, you'll also have no proven track record, no loyal customer base and no previous sales on which to base estimates. The market won't know about you or where to find you. You'll have to learn to do everything by yourself.

## Leasing or Buying a Space

If you have a strong gut feeling about the neighborhood's growth potential, and your gut feeling is backed up by solid, analytical research, a property investment could see a hefty return within a very short time. You'll own the building as well as the boutique business itself, an attractive asset, and a safety net for your business.

"The only real setback I've had in seven years is when the building my boutique is in went up for sale. I had a lease but I didn't own my own space and suddenly I was threatened by the prospect of possibly having to move the business," says Beverly.

### Why Buy?

- It will save money over the long term; rental payments are replaced with mortgage, but mortgage payments eventually result in equity and something you can resell.

- You have more control over how long you can remain in the location and the types of changes you can make to the property.

- You might be able to divide the property and rent part of it to another business tenant, offsetting some of your costs.

- If you choose a neighborhood about to boom, the property will go up in value and you will benefit should you resell (note that it usually takes a while to resell such a major investment, though).

### If You'd Rather Rent

- It will save initial start-up costs since you won't need to factor in a down payment.

- More flexibility — if you need a smaller or larger space later on, it's often easier to end a lease and move on than to try to sell the building.

- Your costs are more predictable. If you own the building and its roof starts to leak, you need to fix it. As a tenant you call the landlord to deal with any structural problems.

- You should be able to claim all of your rent as a tax deduction, whereas if you own the building, depending on local tax laws, you might only be able to claim the interest payments. Ask your accountant about this.

- You'll probably have more choice in location. You might find more spaces for lease than for sale.

There are advantages to both leasing and buying, but the amount of available cash at your disposal will be the major factor in your decision. Buying property in a thriving retail environment is generally an expensive undertaking. You'll need a sizeable deposit and you'll have to plan for a mortgage payment every month.

On the other hand, if you decide to rent, in most cases your start-up investment will require only a month or two in rent to get you going and a security deposit.

## Negotiating a New Lease

When you are ready to start looking, call some commercial real estate agents and tell them what you're looking for in terms of location, exposure and square footage. They'll be able to make appointments for you to view a number of different spaces and will take you around on tours. Ask them as many questions as you want to. As professionals, it's their job to help educate you about commercial properties. They can explain the advantages of one location over another.

Although a commercial real estate agent can help advise you on the terms of your lease and might help you negotiate a lease, certainly don't sign anything until you've had your lawyer read the document. The lease is a legally binding contract and as such should be taken seriously. Your lawyer will be able to explain both the landlord's responsibilities and your own.

TIP:    You might do well to spend a bit of money on a lease negotiator. If you find someone with a thorough knowledge of the area you're planning to open in, they'll have a lot of inside information. They should be able to save you money on your lease, over and above what you'll spend on their services.

Your lease will either be based on a fixed amount, a percentage of your sales, or some combination of the two. The percentage-of-sales lease is most common in shopping centers and other planned retail neighborhoods where the landlord is more heavily involved in advertising and promoting the area.

Other terms of the lease will specify the condition of the space and how much in the way of renovation or build-out the landlord will do, and how much of it is your own responsibility. With a turnkey lease, the landlord will look after any construction issues, so all the tenant has to do is unlock the door and move in his furnishings and merchandise to open for business. Other times a landlord will offer you a bare-bones agreement; it's up to you to look after flooring, electrical, lighting, walls, etc. The advantage here is that you can create your boutique pretty much from scratch. Again, this can get a little complicated and you'll want your attorney to explain exactly what the landlord is offering to do, how much of it is up to you, and who pays for what.

Most importantly, no matter how much you love a given space, do not let your emotions talk you into signing for something that is in reality not what you need. It might be pretty close to the sort of building you've always dreamed of for your boutique, but what is the neighborhood like? Is it thriving, or struggling for its last breath? What are the nearby businesses like? Is there any parking in the neighborhood? Is the wiring up to code?

We're not saying don't listen to your emotions. We believe in gut feeling and intuition. But we believe in backing them up with solid research, especially when it comes to making a decision as important as your business's location.

## 3.3.2   Purchase an Existing Boutique

If you can find a viable, established boutique that happens to be for sale, this can be a wise route to pursue. By purchasing an existing boutique, you'll have an established customer base. People will already be in the habit of visiting the shop, even if you change its name.

Alternately, if the previous owner had any negative associations with customers, neighbors or suppliers, you will have to work hard at overcoming them. If there's a negative reputation clinging to the store it might be hard work turning the business 180 degrees, back to a positive image.

By purchasing an established boutique you'll have access to sales figures, customer records and vendor details. If the seller agrees to give you all of her purchasing information, you'll be able to look up previous orders and trace the product's sell-through. The seller might agree to spend the first week or two working with you and training you in all aspects of her business.

Remember that most of the time you won't be buying your building, but merely leasing the space. When you buy an existing business you still have to pay the rent. However you might be able to take over a good lease and get a better deal than if you negotiated a new lease of your own.

Naturally you will sometimes pay more to buy this business initially than you will to start up on your own, but it might be already turning a profit, or at least closer to the point of profitability. The only reason you might get a big discount is when you pick up a boutique on the verge of bankruptcy. Make sure you find out why the business has failed, or you could be wasting your money fighting a losing battle.

You'll have noticed that was a pretty big "if" that started this section off. You have to do some very careful research. You have to ask some straight questions. Put your emotions aside. If you already love the boutique, its hip location and darling décor, put those emotions into a closet, lock the door, and give your wisest friend the key.

## Key Questions to Ask

### Question #1:    Why is this business for sale?

There should be a reasonable and concrete answer the current owner can offer to this question, and it should be something that you think you can overcome. If the business is failing due to circumstances beyond your control, why do you think your luck will be better than the last owner's?

You might already have a gut feeling — a strong, positive one or the kind that leaves you queasy. Pay attention. Back up your intuition by doing research. Ask around to other local businesses and clients, if possible.

### Question #2:  What does the current owner intend to do after the sale?

It might not be so good for your business if the owners plan to open up the same kind of shop just down the block, and will call all the customers to let them know where they are.

Often one of the clauses on the purchase agreement will state that the seller is not allowed to set up a similar business within a defined area for a fixed number of years. This clause will protect you from the previous owner becoming your fiercest competition.

### Question #3:  How much stock or inventory are you buying with the boutique?

What condition is it in? Is it merchandise you would want, that you'd be happy to pay for? Is it current and seasonal? Will you be able to sell it for a profit, or only if you mark it down by 50%? Is it the sort of stock that will appeal to your customer?

Although many retail businesses are sold "lock, stock and barrel," you don't have to buy the previous owner's inventory. Your offer can be for the goodwill, fixtures and equipment alone, in which case she will be responsible for clearing the merchandise from the premises before you take over.

You should also have access to the suppliers' contact information and you can continue buying from them if you want to, once you have updated their credit departments with the new management information. They might want to put you on COD (cash on delivery) for a time unless you can convince them that you're a good credit risk.

### Question #4:  Does the store have a prominent and positive image in the community?

When you buy an existing business you pay for something called "goodwill". This refers to the fact that the business is already well established and known to a solid group of customers who are in the habit of shopping there regularly, and who in theory will continue to support it once it has changed hands.

Watch people come and go at different times of day. Are they the kind of customer you'd hope to attract yourself? Are they walking out with purchases? Watch the current manager and his staff interact with customers. You might feel funny about this, but you're just protecting your investment. This is a lot of money we're talking about — your money.

---

### A Buyout Success Story

In 1992, Sue was working in a specialty boutique when her employers made a series of bad decisions. She knew that the business had strong potential and felt certain that she could do a better job of running the shop.

She was in the fortunate position of having access to the sales figures. The previous owners weren't reinvesting in the business, and when sales leveled off their expenses continued to increase. Soon they lacked the cash reserves to pay their debts.

"I looked at the numbers and saw that sales were good. The previous owners had mismanaged the business, forgetting the basics of cash flow. I felt sure that I could make it a success," says Sue.

"We bought four stores for $20,000 a store and picked up the stock at fifty cents a unit," she remembers. "The leases were transferred free and clear and we got the mailing lists, too. We were lucky to pick up a viable business at a bargain-basement price."

Sue and her three partners chose to buy the chain of four existing stores and within very little time, she was proven correct. A year after taking over she had turned it into a profitable business by putting profit back into the business to fund its growth.

Thirteen years later Sue and her remaining partner have bought the other two original partners out. They currently run seven shops, ranging from 1300 square feet to 2400 square feet.

---

### Question #5: How long has the boutique been in business?

Does the sales history show a steady, healthy increase? What merchandise category shows the most growth? Has the owner kept good customer files for your reference? Can she show you something that indicates the percentage of returns?

Does the owner have a good relationship with her vendors? Customers? Landlord? Neighbors? How is her credit rating? To an extent, any problems she had will become yours when you take over her business. Make sure you know what you're getting into. Especially if it seems to be doing well on the surface, look carefully into the financial statements, and unless you're already a genius with a profit-and-loss statement, have your accountant look them over, too.

## 3.3.3 Start a Franchise Boutique

Franchising allows you to own your own business while benefiting from the high-profile image and marketing advantages of a large organization. If you are eager to open your own boutique but are concerned about how much work is involved in getting everything set up, or are concerned about the riskiness of an untested business venture, you may want to consider franchising.

Franchising happens when an established company allows someone to run a local business using its company name, logo, products, services, marketing, and business systems. In a franchise relationship, the franchisor is the company who owns a distribution channel of boutiques and often the brand associated with the store; the franchisee is the owner of any individual given store in the group.

Let's say I start up a very successful sandwich shop. People talk about my sandwiches, and more and more customers find their way to me because of my specific recipe, the environment I've created and my presentation. I could choose to come up with enough money to open locations all over the country, or I could start a franchise where I let other people purchase the right to sell my famous sandwiches.

I used the sandwich example because franchising is much more common in the world of fast food than the apparel business. However, there are a few boutique franchise options that are open to you.

## Deciding if a Franchise Suits You

People who choose to franchise rather than start their own boutique from scratch often do so because they want to minimize their risk. They see the franchise as a proven business that already has name recognition among the public. By working with an established system, franchisees hope to avoid costly mistakes and make a profit more quickly.

Franchises are also good for people who have less business know-how, and want support. Franchisors typically provide training to help franchisees start, market and run their new business. The franchisee may receive assistance in everything from obtaining inventory to setting up record-keeping systems.

It is important to keep in mind that a franchisee does not own any of the company's trademarks or business systems. Also, a franchisee must run his or her business according to the terms of the agreement with the franchisor. For example, the franchisee may not be permitted to offer a sales promotion or use a vendor that has not been authorized by the franchisor. While some people appreciate having such guidelines to follow, if you are an independent person who enjoys taking risks and being spontaneous, you might find owning a franchise to be too restrictive.

Since someone else is ultimately in charge, you may be wondering how having a franchise is different from managing someone else's boutique. In fact, there are significant differences. You have more freedom than an employee would (you might choose your own working hours, for example). And you could ultimately earn much more money than an employee.

> **TIP:** What you receive for your investment varies from franchise to franchise, so make sure you know exactly what you will be buying, since franchising is a long-term relationship. You may want to hire a franchise consultant, or consult with your lawyer and accountant before you sign a franchise contract. You can learn about options for free consultation at **www.franchise-consultation.com**.

Although the franchise itself may be quite successful, there is no guarantee that you will be successful after linking up with them and doing business. You may not get the support you had hoped for from the franchisor, or you might find that the geographic location is not right for the boutique.

## Franchise Costs

On average, a franchise is going to cost you more to start up than an independent boutique, but you are gambling on it helping you make a faster profit. Boutique franchises generally require a minimum investment of $100,000, an average of about $200,000, and for big names, gets into the $500,000-plus range. The initial investment typically includes two components: the payment of a franchise fee, and the balance to cover your start-up costs.

For example, Children's Orchard is a franchise that sells new and used children clothing, toys and accessories. Their franchise fee is $22,500, and they estimate the total start-up costs to range from approximately $70,000 to $155,000. You can see a more detailed breakdown at **www. childrensorchard.com/content/view/21/38/**.

In addition to your initial investment, you can expect to pay the franchisor ongoing royalties, which typically range from 7 to 11 percent of your sales; the exact amount will be determined by the company you franchise with.

## Finding a Franchise

There isn't a ton of boutique franchises open for the public to start up, and of the few most focus on selling used clothing or an exclusive product line.

Here are some websites you can explore — search on the terms "retail," "specialty" and "clothing." Note that the companies listed here are provided as examples only, and are not endorsed or recommended. Only you can decide which franchise, if any, is right for you:

- *Canadian Business Magazine 1-Minute Franchise Finder*
  **www.1minutefranchisefinder.com**

- *Best Franchise Opportunities*
  **www.bestfranchiseopportunities.com**

- *Opportunity Expo Retail Clothing Franchises*
  **http://opportunityexpo.com/retail-clothing.php**

- *Business Nation Franchises & Businesses For Sale*
  **www.businessnation.com/franchises/pages/**

## 3.3.4   Non-Traditional Options

If the costs of setting up a retail space are more than you can afford right away, consider launching your boutique as a small kiosk (retail booth), by catalog, or online only. You may find that these non-traditional "locations" are the best long-term fit for your boutique concept, or you can use them as a stepping stone to a brick-and-mortar store.

## Kiosks

There is a cost-effective solution that puts you, literally, in the center of the action in a retail mall: a kiosk, one of those portable retail outlets that we've all watched become a permanent fixture in malls across North America. Today, they're a $10 billion industry.

The kiosk concept owes its success to a formula that pleases both mall owners and entrepreneurs: mall owners get to lease formerly unusable space and make more money, and retailers with limited start-up cash get a great, high-traffic location at a fraction of the cost.

A kiosk also offers great flexibility. Most malls will rent kiosks and carts by the week, even by the day, which gives you the chance to use your time and money wisely. For those selling seasonal merchandise, a kiosk allows you to strategically increase your overhead only in times when you know the potential for a return will be there.

Renting a kiosk, or a scaled-down version called a "cart," will cost you between $2,000 and $10,000 monthly. Mall management also generally requires a one-time fee for new retailers ($500 - $2,000), which covers storage fees and the cost of building or renovating a kiosk to suit your needs.

When renting a kiosk, location should be given the same attention that you would give to leasing storefront property. First, the mall has to be right for your boutique, and attract the demographic that you're trying to sell to. Within the mall, choose a high-traffic location if possible, near entranceways and exits or anchor stores.

> **TIP:** You can also try to set up your kiosk near retail outlets whose products complement yours. When you're located outside a shoe store, you might interest someone in a handbag to match those new shoes.

Contact mall management to inquire about renting a kiosk. They will either have someone on staff who coordinates these deals, or they will direct you to the management company in charge. For other spaces that have kiosks, such as airports and street-level retail, contact the airport or city authority respectively.

Kiosk Marketplaceat **www.kioskmarketplace.com** is the premier information site on kiosk retail.

## Catalogs

Although the catalog has declined in popularity over the last decade, retailers and other companies, including Internet retailers, are rediscovering the power of the catalog as a sales medium.

The appeal of a catalog is the same today as it was a century ago: catalogs have a long "shelf life." A catalog will sit on a coffee table for months, constantly enticing the reader, whereas a flyer will be in the recycling bin faster than an empty milk jug. Also, it allows people to shop from home, and browse from their kitchen table or couch.

While you could operate a catalog-only boutique, in today's marketplace you will likely find that a combined catalog/website, catalog/kiosk, or even catalog/boutique location is more effective than selling by catalog itself, unless you have a reliable list of people to distribute catalogs to.

For a professional-looking catalog, the job of producing your catalog will most likely fall to a professional printer. They will take care of design and printing, and what you provide is the text, photographs and special graphics, such as a company logo. You'll also choose the predominant colors and number of pages.

Prices for catalogs will vary based on the paper you use, the number of colors, and the number of pages. For a general example, the online printer **CatalogPrintingExperts.com** advertises that they will create 5,000 16-page catalogs for about $2,700.

Creating a catalog is only one aspect of this boutique option — the other is distribution. If you choose to send catalogs all at once through the mail, the postal service will often provide a discount on bulk deliveries. Other delivery options include a professional delivery service, which can be found in your Yellow Pages, or you can hit the pavement yourself and go door to door.

## Online Boutiques

Another location option for your boutique is to take your boutique online. Online retail exploded in the 1990s, and is expected to continue to grow. You will still need to find suppliers and will have the added challenge of shipping merchandise, but you will not need to cover the monthly overhead of a physical space.

Not surprisingly, a good website will be the key to success for your online boutique. Shoppers will want to be able to view clear, detailed pictures of the merchandise, be able to read garment details and size availability, calculate accurate shipping costs, and purchase with security and simplicity. Since they can't handle or try on a garment, you'll need to provide enough details to sell the garment by image only.

For these reasons, having a professionally designed website is a necessity. Pricing varies, with most web designers charging by the page, or in a package deal that includes the cost of operation, such as hosting and buying a domain name. In the end, expect to pay an up-front cost between $1,000 and $10,000.

> TIP: You'll want your online boutique to be uncluttered, easily navigated, and have a color scheme that matches that of the one you've chosen for your overall business look. You can read more about setting up an eye-catching website in section 5.5.5 of this guide.

The most important content will be the photographs and descriptions of the garments. Photos of clothing should be taken from several angles and, if possible, they should be both on their own, as well as shown on models. The photos should be accompanied by detailed descriptions of the items, including sizes, colors, material, cleaning directions, and delivery options.

Online boutiques also require a "shopping cart" component. A shopping cart is a tab that customers click on to be taken to an order form to purchase items. The online boutique is notified via email that a purchase has been made, and all the pertinent purchase information and notice of payment is delivered. An automated response will also be sent to the customer.

Online shopping is really the domain of two main payment options: credit cards and PayPal. Credit card payment acceptance is handled through your bank or a merchant service company. Your web designer should have all the details you need, and in the meantime, you can check out Yahoo's Small Business Merchant Solutions at **http://smallbusiness. yahoo.com/ecommerce/**.

PayPal is an online payment service in which money is directly transferred from bank accounts to Paypal and PayPal to bank accounts. It's easy to use and the cost for businesses and consumers is minimal. For information, visit **www.paypal.com**.

The last step to setting up your online boutique is determining how to get the garments ordered to your customers. Post offices and private delivery services offer business rates to help keep shipping costs low. With this said, many online retailers either build the price of shipping into the price of an item, or make shipping costs the responsibility of the consumer.

# 3.4 Your Business Plan

You wouldn't think of building a house without a blueprint to describe the building materials and layout of the rooms, and detail where the plumbing and electricity was needed. The blueprint would communicate your ideas to the contractors and designers, and clarify your own thinking before you start to build.

A business plan for your boutique is much like the blueprint for building a house, except that it consists mostly of words and numbers and doesn't necessarily need any drawings at all. It considers as many aspects of your new business as possible.

Some experts have suggested that you could easily spend a year researching and writing your plan. Don't worry; while that amount of time could produce an amazing plan, it's possible to cut that time significantly if you have done much of the preparation outlined in this guide.

## 3.4.1 Why Have a Plan

If you require financing from a lending institution, or even a friend or relative, a business plan will give them the information they need to consider your request. It will also show that you are a well-organized planner who has given serious attention to the project that they might be about to invest significant amounts of money in.

Even if you don't require outside financing, take time to develop a business plan, and give it just as much attention as if you were taking it to your bank. Developing a business plan will encourage you to clarify many aspects of your venture, and plan ahead for contingencies that you might not have otherwise foreseen. You may have a perfect vision of what you want in your head, but if you don't put it down on paper for others to see, you risk serious miscommunication that could be costly — or "fatal" — to your boutique.

The business plan can start off as a general idea; a direction you want to head in; the concepts and ideas your business will be based on. Be as specific as you can while leaving room for changes as your boutique comes to life.

Your business plan will detail the contacts available to help and advise you, and the opportunities you might be in a unique position to pursue. It will also factor in the current and anticipated market conditions regarding retail outlooks and consumer confidence.

It is important to note that a business plan is an evolving document. Though the concept and foundation of the business may stay the same, the marketing, operations and financials evolve as you learn more about how your business grows and makes money.

## 3.4.2   Parts of the Plan

Now, let's walk through each section of your business plan and how it should be written.

## The Executive Summary

The most frequently read part of your business plan will be the executive summary. It gives potential investors a "snapshot" or concise overview of your idea and why it's a money-maker, and is an enticement to read the rest of your plan.

The executive summary is most often two or three pages of overview on the key elements of your business. Your summary should include all the elements of your business plan, summarized into concise paragraphs. Then the complete business plan is an elaboration on each of those sections with additional detail and your complete set of financials. Your executive summary will read a bit like this:

> The Barefoot Boutique will offer better-quality swimwear to tourists and the residents of the affluent White Sands neighborhood. The boutique will be situated on Marine Drive right across from White Sands Beach, between the large resort Sandcastles and the Bayview Hotel. Visitors will come from the many hotels, inns and bed & breakfast establishments in the area.
>
> A space of 1000 square feet will feature upscale designer swimwear for women, men and children. The area has a significant tourist trade and most retailers on Marine Drive have consistently seen upwards of $750,000 in annual sales. A three-year lease will cost $1,500 per month plus utilities.
>
> The sole proprietor gained experience working in a women's clothing boutique part time while she was at university, has $45,000 of her own to invest in the business, and requires financing of $110,000.

TIP:   You don't really need to sit down and "write" an executive summary. Write the rest of your business plan first, and then use a highlighter to go through and pick out the key details. When you do your summary, you can "cut and paste" directly from the rest of the plan.

# Company Description

In concise language, explain your boutique concept. What are you called, what do you sell, and what makes you unique? You can break this section down into the nature of the business (a few paragraphs on the market niche your boutique will fill), and unique competencies (why your location and plan is perfect).

Use straightforward language to describe your business in positive terms that will give a clear picture of your boutique. You need to prove to potential financiers that you have put a lot of thought into your business and its chances for success.

Get the reader's attention with a clear and detailed discussion of your boutique concept and the specific niche you have in mind. Do not assume that the reader knows much about boutiques in general, fashion or even retail. For example:

> At 1000 square feet, The Barefoot Boutique is a cozy and intimate swimwear shop. The location is a turn-of-the-century heritage building, and the store itself used to be a dress shop.
>
> Most of the stock will be women's suits, with a small collection of men's trunks and children's swimsuits. We'll carry a selection of different styles but will not buy more than one piece of each size or color per design.
>
> The small scale of the store and the flexible buying plan will allow management to monitor changes in the market and its reaction to our product line. We will be able to adapt as necessary and will change our merchandising strategy as we see fit.
>
> Situated at Marine Drive and Calmer Way, the shop is easily accessed by traffic in both directions because of the left-turning lane from Marine onto Calmer. The store will be an easy walk from most of the hotels and resorts in the area. Most visitors will pass by it on their way to and from the beach each day, as well as in the evening on their way to popular restaurants such as The Ginger Pear and Felicity's.

# Market Analysis

This section offers you the opportunity to prove to the reader how much you already know about your industry. You'll want to use statistics about where the fashion or retail industry currently stands (annual revenues and significant trends) and how these numbers support your unique concept. Consulting the North American Industry Classification System will give you an Industry Code you can use to look up predicted growth trends published by the U.S. government for specific industries.

You can use the techniques described in section 4.1.1 of this guide on demographics, as well as reading business magazines and the financial section of the newspaper for economic forecasts, consumer confidence indexes, and trend forecasting.

Industry publications are also beneficial because the articles in them are geared towards business people like yourself. There is an extensive list of professional associations and publications at the end of this guide you can check out to see which are the best fit for what you plan to sell.

Don't exaggerate or make assumptions; instead, cite the most reliable sources of data you have access to. Here is a sample of typical language in this section:

> The permanent population of the area known as White Sands is about 30,000, a figure that quadruples between the months of May and September. The Barefoot Boutique expects to do 70% of its annual sales within these five months, and we will extend our hours during this peak season to accommodate the growth in business.
>
> The White Sands area has experienced significant tourist trade growth in the last three years, according to the local Chamber of Commerce. Most retailers on Marine Drive have consistently seen upwards of $750,000 in annual sales, reflecting a 200% growth from five years ago. Number of visitors has also increased sharply in recent times, as demonstrated in the graph below…

## Customer Profile

Here you prove to the reader that you know who your market is going to be. What sex are they? What age demographic, what education level do they typically have? What do you know about their current buying habits? How much disposable income do they have and how do they tend to spend it? What do you know about their careers or lifestyles?

An estimated 80% of our customers will be tourists staying at the 46 hotels, B&Bs and resorts in the area. The balance will live in the affluent areas of White Rock, the Bluffs and Windy Bay that surround White Sands. We expect 80% of our buyers to be women, even when the purchase is for a child's or men's swimsuit.

Information provided from the local Chamber of Commerce suggests that both types of customers have family incomes in excess of $100,000. Most have university educations and either own their own businesses or have professional occupations.

More than two thirds of the residents of the neighborhoods mentioned take at least two annual vacations to a beach resort. About half of the houses have pools of their own and 86% have memberships to a health club with swimming and/or whirlpool facilities.

## Competitive Strategy

This particular section of your plan will explain to readers what makes you different from your competition. In one sense, your competition is any retail outlet within a certain geography who sells the same line of DKNY jeans and sportswear that you stock. This might include department stores, discount outlets and Internet vendors.

In another sense, your competition is the local retailers who are carrying the lines that compete with DKNY – in other words anybody who's selling designer jeans and sportswear to your chosen demographic.

"In a small community like Port Townsend, every other business retailing clothing, whether new or secondhand, is my competition. That includes the thrift store down the street," says Beverly.

If you aren't sure who will be selling the same products as you, try calling a supplier you hope to use. A good supplier will be careful not to saturate a small region with too much of the same product, so before you place an order you can ask who else in your area carries the same line.

In this section you can explain what the other stores look like, where they advertise, what their hours of operation are, their exchange policies, etc. Explain what are they doing right, and how you will do this even better. Explain what are they doing wrong, and how you will use this as leverage for your business. For example:

> There are no exclusive swimwear shops on Marine Drive. The women's store Swan Song carries a limited selection of ladies' swimsuits, but this is three blocks from Marine Drive, away from the beach, on Crescent Avenue. To buy men's swimsuits, children's suits or any designer-label suits one currently has to go all the way into Woodland Hills. Swan Song carries no sarongs, cover-ups or beach footwear.

Your competitive strategy should also focus on the following:

- Will your pricing be higher or lower than your competitors and why?
- What features are highlighted in your business (hard-to-find product, superior service)?

What special features of your boutique will draw customers into your shop instead of the competition two blocks away? The answer to this could be something unique about the product you carry, your pricing structure, the way it's displayed or the level of personal service you offer. It could be the lighting and music in your boutique that creates a hip, cool ambiance that is especially desirable to your target market. It could even be all of the above.

## Marketing Strategy

The marketing strategy section explains how you will let your market know about your business. This is the place to address your corporate identity, brand, advertising and promotion campaign, exposure in the neighborhood, Internet presence, etc.

Explain why your boutique is ideally situated to reach these customers. Chances are they live, work and/or go to school in the neighborhood. Go into the logistics of how you plan to let the market know about your boutique through signage, window displays, advertising, promotions, press kits, etc.

How will you create a buzz about your boutique and get people eagerly anticipating your grand opening? Will you paint your car and your spouse's car with the store name and logo to create awareness, or flyer the cars parked in the immediate vicinity?

Will you have a grand opening weekend, a fashion show, a customer referral program, a website, or just a listing in the Yellow Pages? You can read over the marketing ideas in section 5.5 to get your creative juices flowing.

---

Marketing and advertising will focus on reaching both the visitors and the local population. The owner has just purchased a Daimler Chrysler Smart car and intends to logo it to generate interest and awareness.

Print advertising will appear in the local magazine The Driftwood during the tourist season. We'll offer guests of the Bayview and diners at Felicity's a coupon offering 10% off their first purchase, and we will circulate free postcards for people to send home. These will feature photographs of models wearing our suits. The cards will be available at cafés and bookstores through the area, and will feature our website address as well as physical address, phone and fax.

We will have a web-catalog enabled for e-commerce to offset slower sales in the winter season and to overcome the fact that many of our customers may not return to the area for a holiday again, but having seen our store and our selection would like to shop with us again.

Press releases will advise the media of our grand opening in May, which will feature an in-store fashion show. After that each season will feature a fashion show to exhibit the newest styles to our community. Store bags will be of stiff glossy paper, with cord handles. Bags and gift boxes will be blue and white, printed with our logo and web address.

---

## Merchandise

Describe the merchandise lines that you'll carry in detail. Don't just say "women's clothing," but pin down whether it's trendy and inexpensive, basic, classic, expensive and higher quality, or designer wear that combines the timely aspects of high fashion with an up-market price.

What is the average retail price point of your product? Will you focus on evening wear, perhaps, or casual clothing, or plus-size career wear? Mention a few of the better-known labels that you will carry. Even if you plan to start a secondhand designer boutique with clothing acquired by consignment, you can list the labels that you'll be looking for. How much opening inventory in dollars you expect to need? (We'll help you figure this one out in section 4.3).

> The Barefoot Boutique will sell medium to high-end bathing suits, sarongs and cover-ups. Labels will include major sportswear manufacturers like Fila and Roxy, as well as designer brands like Calvin Klein and Ralph Lauren.
>
> Swimsuits will comprise about 60% of the retail value of the stock, with sarongs and cover-ups taking an additional 20%. The remaining 20% will be a selection of flip-flops and slip-on surf shoes, sunhats, glasses, accessories and beach towels.

## Store Operations

Explain in this section how you will run your boutique. Detail the square footage of your proposed location, the look of the store, your hours of operation, and your number of employees, as well as any plans for future expansion.

If you have them (and it will look far more professional if you do), you can also include:

- An operations manual and/or employee manual

- A list of your planned starting inventory mix

- A detailed list of your equipment and supplies

If you already have a space in mind, describe the property itself and go into the specifics of your lease, as well as the licenses and permits required by the municipality.

Detail the building itself, the size of your space in square feet, the type of public access, windows, parking, etc. Describe the store front as it is now and as it will be when open for business. Include a photo of the existing building if it looks attractive or shows obvious potential.

The corner location will attract traffic from both Marine Drive and the adjacent Calmer Way, and the front door is angled under a dome-shaped awning, creating a welcoming feeling from both directions. There are three customer parking spots in the rear of the building and additional parking on the street out front. Large windows face both streets and will be changed weekly to display new product.

The stucco exterior will be painted a sea-blue, with the front door a contrasting white. There are Italian terra cotta containers on either side of the front door planted with topiary bay trees and lavender. Signage will be a crisp white background with the logo and the name in dark blue script. The original pine plank floors will be left their natural, sandy color and the walls will be painted a pale turquoise.

Fixtures such as rods, racks and shelving are the same natural wood shade. The cash desk at the back of the store is also varnished wood with a glass inset that opens into an area for displaying sunglasses and small accessories.

There are two fitting rooms with full-length mirrors and natural wood saloon-style doors opening out into the store. Behind the cash desk and the fitting rooms, a door leads into a back room large enough for receiving stock, with a staff lunch table and a washroom.

The interior design details will be contracted by retail specialists H.I. Linden and Associates, who designed the successful unisex boutique Now in nearby Woodland Hills.

May through September, The Barefoot Boutique will be open from 10 a.m. until 9 p.m. daily. The additional staff required will be one full-time and two part-time salespeople. All will have previous retail experience, preferably in apparel, and will undergo a training program to increase their selling and customer service skills.

During the shoulder season (March-April and October-December) hours will be Tuesday through Sunday, noon to 8 p.m. During this quieter period we will only require the sole proprietor and one part-time sales person.

Much of the Marine Drive retail community shuts down in January and February, but the Barefoot Boutique will be open from Tuesday to Sunday, noon to 6:00 p.m. We recognize that this is the time of year when most of the local residents go on vacation to the South Pacific or the Caribbean, and our research indicates that many of them purchase at least one new swimsuit before their trip.

> We'll need two phone lines, one for voice calls and one for fax and debit machines. The computerized cash and inventory control system will be the Dinger XT-5000, with an alarm and security monitoring provided by Alarm Experts.

## Management and Ownership

This section will encompass everything from the big picture of your business to its daily operations. Your plan should outline the management structure. Will you be both owner and manager? Will you hire a manager or an assistant manager?

This is also your opportunity to sell yourself and your relevant experience. Be forthright about why you think you can be a success at running this boutique. If you have experience running previous businesses, be sure to highlight this fact. A proven track record in business will strengthen your credibility and increase interest from lenders and investors.

> The sole proprietor has managed a real estate firm for the past four years, and during this time has been responsible for maintaining the company's website. She also worked at Cottonental Drift part-time when she was in university, a women's boutique whose market was primarily college students and young women, located in a residential neighborhood south of Woodland Hills. She learned good selling skills and gained familiarity with the basics of running a boutique.

## Financial Data

If you are seeking funding, your business plan should conclude with a statement of the total dollar amount you want to borrow, both immediately and over the next five years.

It should also state what you plan to use those funds for, and outline your long-term financial strategies that may require more funding down the road, such as expansion of your boutique, building another location, etc. Section 3.5.3 has more information on planning a startup budget for your boutique.

For some people this is the least fun aspect of thinking about a new business. For lenders and investors, however, this is the most important part of the plan. These financial documents provide evidence that you have thought your plan through, accounted for all expenses, and most importantly to banks and investors, that you have a solid process in place to pay back lenders.

You will also include some details of assumptions you have based your calculations on, since nobody knows exactly what the future will bring in terms of economy and other factors.

The financial statements should indicate how much capital of your own you're putting into the business and how much additional capital will be required. You should detail what you're going to do with that capital; how much of it will be invested in equipment and supplies versus things like rent and promotions.

List the cash register and/or computer, phones and fax machines, furnishings for the storeroom and fitting rooms and any fixtures such as shelving and racks. Decide how many hangers, gift boxes and shopping bags you'll need, and where you'll order them from.

They'll expect you to stick to this budget, too. If you budget $1,500 for grand opening publicity and $50,000 for opening inventory, lenders will be displeased later to see that you actually spent $5,000 on a grand opening party and $45,000 for inventory.

The elements of your plan will indicate at what point you expect to turn a profit, and how much your profit or loss will be for the first year and in each consecutive year (it is not unusual for a business to budget for a loss in year one, due to start-up costs).

Projecting your first year's sales is a difficult thing to do because there are so many variables and you'll have no history to go by unless you're purchasing an existing business.

For a 1000 square foot store, the people interviewed for this book suggested your sales for that first year could be anywhere from $60,000 to $200,000, and of course your figures might be even less than that on the low end. It's going to depend on your product, your location, how much of your market finds its way to your boutique, advertising, the local economy, etc.

"When you do your calculations, use a variety of projections to figure out that break-even point. Start with what you think annual sales might be, and then try another figure. 'Okay, what if sales were $10,000 less. Would I still make it?' That way you're prepared for different scenarios," advises boutique owner Beth.

You should outline your basic bookkeeping method and your plan for keeping payroll and other records. Include copies of any loan applications already filed. You will want to hire a qualified accountant, ideally with retail experience, to assist you in the preparation of these documents.

The key word here is assist. You should be involved in this process, even if the very word accounting inspires a great big yawn. As the business owner, you should have at least a passing familiarity with these numbers, where they come from, and the story they tell about the state of your business.

## Other Parts of Your Plan

- *A cover sheet:* The plan should be introduced by a cover sheet that in one page or less simply states the objective of your boutique and a summary of the key points. Make sure it has your contact details and invite prospective lenders to call you with any questions.

- *Table of contents:* A brief table of contents should follow the cover, listing elements of the business plan and what pages each section starts on. Use major headings and subheadings to identify content.

- *Other supporting documents:* These might include your resume, your tax returns for the last three years, a personal financial statement (the form can be obtained from your bank), a copy of the franchise contract (if relevant) with any franchisor's documents, a copy of a proposed lease or purchase agreement for your space, licenses, permits and any other legal documents, and letters of intent from suppliers.

### 3.4.3   Business Plan Resources

There are a number of free online resources that you can use to help you write a more professional business plan for your new venture. Another option is to invest in business plan software that allows you to input your information into a ready-made template.

Many entrepreneurs use the United States Small Business Administration (SBA)'s business plan outline as a model when writing this document. You can find it at **www.sba.gov/smallbusinessplanner/plan/ writeabusinessplan**. The Canada Business Service Centres (CBSC) also provides a sample business plan and other helpful resources at **http:// bsa.canadabusiness.ca**.

American Express offers a user-friendly guide at **www133.american express.com/osbn/tool/biz_plan/index.asp**. The American Express site will actually let you practice writing a plan for a fictitious business. This will be a very helpful exercise before you get ready to prepare your own plan.

As mentioned earlier, the Service Corps of Retired Executives (**www. score.org**) has volunteers throughout the U.S. who donate time to mentor small businesses free of charge. Their website also has helpful articles to guide you through the process.

You can also use business planning software to help you with your business plan. The most popular program on the market is Palo Alto's Business Plan Pro. It features step-by-step instructions for creating your plan, and has hundreds of business plan templates that you can edit and customize for your own business. You can buy Business Plan Pro for about $100 at **www.paloalto.com**.

## 3.5   Start-up Costs and Funding

Coming up with the finances to open your own business may seem like a daunting proposition, but starting a boutique can be done on a relatively small scale. There are numerous ways to keep your costs manageable and we'll discuss many of them in this section. The key word here is "relatively"; this isn't going to be a nickel-and-dime operation. It's very important to understand that adequate financing is a vital component to your success. Our experts agreed that you can't start a boutique with too much money, but you can try to do it for too little.

Don't be too conservative when you estimate your start-up costs, as it's commonly said that one of the number-one reasons for failure in any kind of business is under-financing. Some things can't be done right on a shoestring.

## 3.5.1   What to Expect

So, how much will it cost you to start a boutique of your own? Of course, that depends. The numbers are going to vary widely depending on a number of factors, but you can probably count on a minimum of $50,000 to open a boutique with new merchandise.

That figure could easily jump up to $250,000 if you have champagne tastes and lofty aspirations, but on the other hand if you can take your inventory on consignment instead of purchasing it, you'll be whittling the low end of the range down a bit more. One of our boutique owners suggested that in certain markets you could open a used-clothing boutique at an extreme low-end cost of $5,000 these days.

Wendy opened her consignment boutique in 1993 for a total of $7,000, with new product and a prime location. Her store was located in a high-traffic, alternative neighborhood in downtown Vancouver. The money came from her grandfather, so she didn't have to borrow anything to start up.

Two things kept her costs down. The first was that she got stock on consignment from local designers, so she didn't have to pay for any merchandise up front. The other thing was that she and her husband were pretty handy and willing to learn to do the things they didn't already know how to do. Together they did the necessary renovations to the shop. "It would cost a lot more to do it today," she points out, "but you learn to work within whatever budget you're given."

## 3.5.2   Factors That Affect Cost

So, if money is an issue, and for most of us it is, how can you keep start-up costs down realistically? The amount you'll need depends primarily on the following three factors:

- Location/build-out

- Style of merchandise

- New product or consignment

## Location and Build-out

It obviously will cost you more to open up a boutique in Manhattan than it will in Bozeman, Montana. Even within your chosen town or city, some of the neighborhoods or shopping centers will have much higher rents than others. Remember that before you jump to sign the lease for the least expensive property you look at, the higher-rent areas tend to have more passersby with more disposable income. For you, that translates to more customers and more sales.

You can also keep costs down a lot by not going crazy on the build-out. "The quality of merchandise you buy is more important than spending a lot on pretty pink walls," says boutique owner Sue.

## Style of Merchandise

Remember that your start-up costs will have to cover your opening inventory, and starting with a lower-priced line is one way to reduce your costs. If your boutique specializes in T-shirts, the average cost of a garment will be much lower than that of a shop carrying leather coats.

For example, if your opening inventory is 100 T-shirts that cost you $4 each, then your total start-up cost for inventory is $400. If you then choose to sell them for $10 each, and you don't sell any at a reduced sale price, you will have earned $1,000. Subtract your initial cost of $400, you've made $600 towards paying your operating costs and making a profit.

Now look at the store that opens with 50 leather jackets whose cost is $100 each for a total cost of $5,000. If you choose to sell every piece at $250, you've netted $7,500 towards paying your overhead. That's significantly higher than the T-shirt store's $600.

However, before you commit to opening a leather store or buying a collection of high-end designer dresses, remember that you'd probably

## Other Ways to Cut Costs

The three factors mentioned are the biggest ones to consider when you look at ways to reduce expenses, but naturally you can apply creative thrifty concepts to every decision you make. Those dollars saved will add up to thousands off your start-up costs. For example:

- Purchase secondhand mannequins and store fixtures instead of brand new (don't put them in your window if they are noticeably unattractive, though).

- Do some of the interior design work, like painting, yourself. A handy friend might be able to help you lay laminate flooring in exchange for a discount on purchases later.

- Trade and barter where possible. The printer who does your business cards might give you a reduced rate if you put a link to their business on your website, or allow a space in your grand opening fashion show program for a small advertisement.

- A skilled negotiator might be able to talk the landlord into a reduced rent in exchange for putting a small display that promotes other businesses he or she leases to in a corner of one of your windows. Just make sure that whatever you do to affiliate yourself with the other business is in good taste and doesn't detract from your primary goal of bringing customers into your store.

- Leasing some of your equipment instead of buying it outright is considered a form of financing that can ease the strain of your cash flow. Be aware that it reduces your business assets, which a bank may not like.

- Supply-side financing refers to getting credit from your vendors so you don't have to pay for ordered merchandise as soon as it is received. It's rare for a new business to get much credit from suppliers, but you might be able to negotiate terms of 30 or 60 days. If that happens you'll have had a month or two to sell your stock before you need to pay for it.

take longer to sell 50 leather jackets. It's a balancing act of finding what works for you and your store. We'll take a more detailed look at pricing your merchandise correctly in section 4.4.

## New Product or Consignment

Another way to keep your costs down is to not purchase your inventory outright. This practice is known as consigning, and it is a very common way to run a second-hand or vintage clothing shop. Suppliers will bring their clothing to you and ask you to sell it for them. You sign an agreement to give them a percentage of the sale, only once the piece has sold.

This is a huge break for your budget because you don't have to come up with the cash to buy things outright. The supplier owns her garment until you sell it for her. She can ask to take it back after a few months if it isn't selling. (We'll take a closer look at secondhand and consignment businesses in section 4.3.5.)

Occasionally, very small-scale, new designers might agree to consigning pieces too, as a way to get themselves established. As we mentioned, that's how Wendy managed to start her business for a minimal investment and show a profit every year. Consignment for first-run clothing usually only works with new designers because they need the exposure. Don't even thinking about calling your Calvin Klein sales agent and asking if they'll give you a few pieces on consignment. You'll have the most luck selling this idea to local designers just starting up in your city.

## 3.5.3   Sample Start-up Budget

On the next page is a table suggesting the range of costs associated with each aspect of a new boutique of about 800 square feet, based on information provided by the boutique owners interviewed for this guide, and industry information.

Keep in mind that this is an example only; the high and low end figures are going to vary enormously depending on a number of decisions you make along the way.

## Sample Start-up Budget

| One-Time Expenses | Low End | High End |
|---|---|---|
| * Build-out (renovate, decorate, etc.) | $12,000 | $27,000 |
| ** Opening inventory | 12,000 | 45,000 |
| Fixtures | 4,000 | 10,000 |
| Security deposit | 1,500 | 20,000 |
| Equipment | 1,000 | 4,000 |
| Start-up promotion/advertising | 1,000 | 10,000 |
| Supplies | 400 | 2,000 |
| Legal and accounting | 800 | 1,500 |
| Website design | 500 | 5,000 |
| Permits/licenses | 150 | 400 |
| **TOTALS (Average: $86,625)** | **$33,350** | **$124,900** |

*\* Can be as low as $1,000 for minimal cosmetic work*

*\*\* Can be as low as $0 for a consignment business*

# Working Capital

In addition to the one-time expenses listed above, you will need a certain amount of working capital to cover monthly operating expenses until you have enough of a cash flow to cover these. The number of months you'll need to cover will be based on the projections in your business plan. These expenses will include:

- Rent
- Insurance
- Ongoing advertising and promotions
- Utilities
- Telephone costs

- Accounting

- Owner salary

- Payroll

- Supplies

- Taxes

- Updating your boutique website

While your working capital costs will be specific to your business, our research and experience suggests a range of $5,000 to $50,000 required in working capital for each month following start up that you require it, and an average of about $50,000 for a four-month ramp-up period. You can talk to your lending institution to see if it is possible to have this available as a line of credit, rather than part of your initial on-hand cash.

How long will it take your business to turn a profit? That will depend entirely on how well you manage it, how thrifty you are at reducing unnecessary expenses, and how strong your sales figures are.

Most business owners are reluctant to discuss how much money they're making, but we can tell you that of the people interviewed for this book, three were showing a profit within their first few months of opening, and two took several years to turn a profit. It's fairly likely that your own profitability point will fall somewhere within that (admittedly wide) range.

Also, when calculating how much you'll need to get your business started, be sure to take into account your personal living expenses for at least the first six months and up to the first two years of your business start-up. Things can take some time to get rolling and you don't want to put yourself into a personal financial bind.

## Start-up Budget Worksheet

Below you will find a worksheet for you to use to budget your own start-up costs. Make a few copies of it and complete it with different scenarios as you start looking at different spaces and different lines of stock to carry.

# Sample Start-Up Budget Worksheet

## One-Time Expenses

|  | Amount |
|---|---|
| Build-out *(renovate, decorate, etc.)* | |
| Opening inventory | |
| Fixtures | |
| Security deposit | |
| Equipment | |
| Start-up promotion/advertising | |
| Supplies | |
| Legal and accounting | |
| Website design | |
| Permits/licenses | |
| **Total one-time expenses** | |

## On-Going Expenses

|  | Amount | Months Required | Total |
|---|---|---|---|
| Rent | | | |
| Insurance | | | |
| Advertising and promotions | | | |
| Utilities | | | |
| Telephone costs | | | |
| Accounting | | | |
| Owner salary | | | |
| Payroll | | | |
| Supplies | | | |
| Taxes | | | |
| Website updates | | | |
| **Total on-going expenses** | | | |
| **Total one-time expenses** *(from above)* | | + | |
| **Total start-up expenses** | | = | |

# Sample Equipment and Supplies Checklist

Here is a list of equipment and supplies for your boutique. You can use the checklist to check off equipment and supplies as you buy them, and also early on to estimate equipment/supply start-up costs.

## Staff and Store Room

- ❑ Box cutter
- ❑ Clock
- ❑ Coffeemaker & coffee
- ❑ Cups
- ❑ Doorbell
- ❑ Microwave
- ❑ Moving dolly
- ❑ Paper towels
- ❑ Shelving
- ❑ Shipping boxes
- ❑ Soap
- ❑ Staffroom furniture
- ❑ Store cleaning supplies
- ❑ Washroom supplies
- ❑ Water cooler

## Merchandising

- ❑ Clothes hangers
- ❑ Clothes racks
- ❑ Mannequins
- ❑ Material for display windows

❑ Merchandise tables

❑ Price tags

❑ Sale signs

❑ Seasonal decorations

❑ Steamer

❑ Store fixtures

❑ Store sign

## Point of Sale

❑ Accessory displays

❑ Boxes

❑ Cash register

❑ Cash register software

❑ Cash register tapes

❑ Credit card machine

❑ Debit card equipment

❑ Gift boxes

❑ Kleenex

❑ Paper

❑ Pens

❑ Scissors

❑ Shopping bags

❑ Stapler

❑ Tape

❑ Wrapping paper

## Office

- ❑ Accounting books
- ❑ Accounting software
- ❑ Business cards
- ❑ Computer/printer
- ❑ Day-timer
- ❑ Employee application forms
- ❑ Fax
- ❑ Inventory tracking system
- ❑ Invoices
- ❑ Keys
- ❑ Lamps
- ❑ Order forms
- ❑ Payroll software
- ❑ Photocopier
- ❑ Safe
- ❑ Telephones

## Miscellaneous

- ❑ Alarm system
- ❑ Bar code scanner
- ❑ Bar code software
- ❑ Bar code tickets
- ❑ Benches/stools
- ❑ CDs

- ❏ Digital camera

- ❏ Interior design accessories (plants, paintings)

- ❏ Light bulbs

- ❏ Mirrors

- ❏ Security clothes tags

- ❏ Security mirrors

- ❏ Security system

- ❏ Stereo

# 3.5.4   Financing Your Boutique

Few of us can come up with sufficient money to start a new boutique and keep it afloat on our own. Whether you're building a business from scratch, purchasing an existing store, or buying into a franchise, chances are good that you'll require a cash injection of some sort. So what are your options?

## Your Own Savings and Investments

There are definite advantages to financing your boutique on your own, if you are able to do so. Large interest payments are eliminated from your cash flow outgoings, you're able to maintain more control over your business, and the stress of having to repay investors on schedule is reduced.

While some experts argue that you should always try to invest a financial institution's money rather than your own, for most small business owners, the best advice falls somewhere in the middle.

You should definitely invest some of your own money, but perhaps not every penny that you have in the world. For one thing, lenders will take your business plan more seriously when they see that you're putting your own capital into the project. Another issue is that the less you borrow, the less you will have to repay and the less interest you will incur.

On the other hand, you might not want to drain your life savings and put everything you have into a new venture. If the economy takes a turn for the worse and your business doesn't succeed as planned, you'll take comfort knowing that you left a bit of savings in reserve.

How much capital of your own can you find to invest? There are various assets to turn to. The obvious ones are your cash savings and any investments, stocks or bonds. You might own property that can be liquidated or rented, and if your retirement funds are substantial you could consider dipping into them.

Other options include cash value in insurance policies, holiday homes, boats, fine art and rare antiques, and jewelry. Perhaps you and your spouse don't need that second car. And if you've ever lent money to friends or relatives to start their own business, consider calling in the loans.

It is possible to start a business without going to the bank. "I was able to finance my business from my own savings and the investment of family and friends, and I paid it all off within the first year," says Margaret.

## Family

Your spouse is an obvious choice because he or she will be intimately involved in your business. However, if you ask them to cash in any independent investments and you have already liquidated your own, remember that the two of you will be entirely dependent on your boutique becoming a success. Consider the stress this could put on your relationship.

Your parents, your spouse's parents, grandparents, aunts, uncles and siblings are good candidates too, although this will depend entirely on your own personal family dynamic. Many people would far rather be indebted to a bank at higher interest rates that ask their family for so much as a dime. Your gut feeling as you read this will likely tell you whether it's a good idea to approach family for money.

If you do turn to your family, chances are they'll have your best interests at heart and they might be more indulgent (i.e. generous) than your high-school friend or neighbor will be. Remember also that if they lend (or give!) you a fat stack of cash, they might feel entitled to put in their two cent's worth of opinions about any business decisions you'll make.

## Friends

Unless your best friend has always insisted that she would love to support you in a business venture, tread carefully. Friends are sometimes uncomfortable when they're asked for money, especially money that it might take a while to recover. And even if they hand over a fistful of cash with barely a blink of the eye, imagine for a moment the potential strain on your friendship if it takes you longer than agreed to repay the loan.

If you do ask a friend for money:

- Make sure you're offering a reasonable rate of interest. You should be paying her more than she'd get if she left her money sitting in the bank. Chances are that interest rate will still be far less than what the bank would charge you to borrow, so you're both better off. This rule applies to borrowing from family too, unless they insist otherwise.

- Get it on paper, ideally on a legal form stating that they will not own any interest in your business once the principal and interest have been repaid in full. State what the repayment rate will be, and at what point the loan should be paid off.

- Before you sign the loan agreement, consider what the friendship means to you and how you'd feel if anything went wrong. If she's been your best buddy since kindergarten, you might decide that protecting that special relationship is more important to you than borrowing the money.

## Banks and Credit Unions

Banks love to lend money. That's what they're for. Your bank wants you to succeed and will provide you with a certain amount of advice. Banks are conservative, too. They love to lend money but especially they love to get it back, on time, with a hefty bit of interest thrown in. For most intents and purposes, a credit union operates in much the same way as a bank and offers many of the same services.

Many of them only like to lend a lot of money; anything under a certain figure is such small potatoes it's hardly worth their while. If that's the case they may suggest a line of credit instead of a traditional loan agreement.

They will probably insist on a business plan, personal credit references and credit history and something big, like your house, as collateral. They will probably want to review all financial statements regularly, perhaps even quarterly, and will expect you to make regular payments as agreed. They might also want your credit card business as part of the deal.

## Other Options

### Lending Institutions

There are specific financing companies that will take on those who the banks turn down. They have greater risk tolerance but they do insist on collateral and their interest rates can be very daunting. These firms should be your last resort.

### Venture Capitalists

This type of investor generally looks for growth industries that offer a quick and certain return on their investment. They are rarely interested in the longer term rewards associated with a boutique.

### Government Programs

In the U.S. one of the Small Business Administration's roles is to assist with financing for small businesses by securing loans with lending institutions. You'll find details about their application process at **www.sba.gov/services/financialassistance**. In Canada the Business Development Bank fills a similar role. Visit **www.bdc.ca/en**. Many Canadian provincial governments also have organizations to support small business initiatives. Your local provincial government can direct you to the relevant programs.

Many potential boutique owners are women, and if you fall into that category in the U.S.A. you should consider the Online Women's Business Center. Visit **http://www.sba.gov/aboutsba/sbaprograms/onlinewbc**.

# 4. Preparing to Open

Starting any business is a life-changing event, and a boutique is no different. Once you have decided to take the plunge, you will be thrust into the excitement, the challenges, and the hectic pace of keeping your opening on schedule.

This chapter of the guide is designed to prepare you for the many decisions that will be a part of planning to launch your boutique, right up to the first day you open your doors for business.

## 4.1 Choose a Location

We've already stressed the importance of location. Let's say it once more. The location you choose is fundamental to your boutique's success.

Remember, location means not only the city you choose for your boutique, but also the neighborhood, the street, and even the specific address on that street. It means who your neighboring businesses are, the schools within a few blocks, the residential properties and the parking available. These are all part of the equation.

We suggest that you do your research thoroughly and use a logical, analytical process rather than let your emotions sway you. This section will discuss all of the issues you'll need to consider in your quest for the ultimate address.

## 4.1.1   Demographics

Demographics simply means the characteristics of a particular segment of the population, and you will want to thoroughly research the demographics of the area where you are considering opening your boutique.

If you find that the segment of the population that you want to target isn't readily available in your area, you may need to shift your focus to a different group. Don't open up a children's wear boutique in a community where everyone is in their sixties and not having too many babies.

Knowing where you stand is far better than building your business on guesses, so do your research. Inquire at the local Chamber of Commerce, whose function is to assist new businesses with questions about the community. You can find your local chamber of commerce at **www. chamberofcommerce.com**.

You can also use census information to find out about potential neighborhoods. Visit **www.census.gov** for U.S. information or **www.statcan. ca** for Canadian information.

You can also try the city's Trade and Convention Center or Visitors' Bureau, and your bank's small business center for demographic information, and community newspapers, which offer a cross-section of ads for local businesses and information about residents.

Demographic information can be obtained in more "grassroots" ways too. Chat to people in the neighborhood café. Ask them how business is, whether there has been much crime in the area, or if they've heard about any new developments going up.

TIP: If something negative comes up that is planned for nearby, though, don't rely on hearsay. You should go to your city planning department and find out about development plans, proposed changes to traffic patterns, etc.

Ask questions like the following to dig into the demographics of towns and communities you are considering locating in.

## What does the population look like?

- Are they mostly single young professionals? Good place to open up a boutique offering designer club-wear.

- Are they young families? Think children's and maternity wear potential.

- Are they empty-nesters? With the kids grown and out of the house, these couples will spend more on themselves and on travel.

## Average family income and common professions?

If you plan to offer a high-end product, your demographic will need a certain combined family income to achieve the disposable income that will make them likely customers. If 80% of the town's population was employed by a lumber mill that just shut its doors, don't opt for the designer shop.

Nor would you open a discount outlet in a neighborhood where the houses are all mansions surrounded by high walls and gates. The people who live in those mansions are not your customers. They buy their designer clothing at exclusive shops, not discount outlets. They will be more motivated by the prestige of a high-end shop than saving a few dollars that they don't actually need.

## Does the area have a significant number of students?

If so, most of them will have limited cash to spend on clothing, so you might not want the shop to be too high-end. On the other hand, they're usually fashion-conscious and like to shop. Well-priced, youthful boutiques with contemporary styles can do well in college towns. Of course, if the local college is an Ivy League school for more privileged students, they won't be as conscious of their budgets.

If you do open up on a block that seems quite busy but has a lot of struggling students in the neighborhood, and the cafés are all value-oriented, you should make sure your boutique won't ask customers to part with a lot of their cash. Maybe a consignment boutique that sells cool "new-to-you" clothing would do well, or a fun accessories place where they can walk out with a great scarf for less than ten dollars, or a groovy T-shirt shop.

## What are the recreational activities enjoyed by people in the community?

Swimsuit stores are perfect for beach communities. Cozy après-ski attire would be a good bet for a mountain resort. If the area is surrounded by golf courses, a casual golf-attire boutique could be a great success.

---

## Questionnaire for Potential Neighborhoods

What is the population of the area?

_____

_____

How does that figure compare to five years ago? Is it growing, or fading out?

_____

_____

Does the residential population consist mainly of families or single people?

_____

_____

How many young children or teenagers live in the area?

_____

_____

What is the average household income?

_____

_____

What is the typical economic status of the neighborhood?

_____

_____

---

Are most people employed, or do they own a business?

_____

_____

What type of professions are most common?

_____

_____

Does most of the adult population have some post-secondary education?

_____

_____

How many own a second home, investment property, summer cottage, etc.?

_____

_____

Do most of the residents drive or do they cycle, take transit, etc.?

_____

_____

Do they own their home or car?

_____

_____

More than one car per household?

_____

_____

How many families take regular annual vacations?

_____

_____

How many belong to fitness clubs or country clubs?

_____

_____

How often does the average family dine out?

_____

_____

How many have season tickets to the theater, opera, ballet or symphony?

_____

_____

Does the area have a university, college or technical school?

_____

_____

Does it support a significant student population?

_____

_____

How many out-of-town tourists typically visit and stay in the area in a given year?

_____

_____

Where are these visitors typically from?

_____

_____

What is the average residential property value in the area?

_____

_____

What percentage of the population is of retirement age?

_____

_____

How many new babies were born to resident families in the past year? The past five years?

_____

_____

## 4.1.2 The Business Mix

Now you've come up with some statistics about the larger community that will be home to your boutique. Your research isn't over. Are you going to settle down in the city center, its primary business district, or somewhere a little more out of the way? Even small towns usually have a variety of shopping areas that offer advantages and disadvantages.

# Shopping Centers

There's no question that being in a shopping center has its advantages for the boutique owner and the customer. They are weatherproof, air-conditioned and out of the sun on the hottest days, and warm and dry during the inclement winter months. Foot traffic numbers tend to be consistently high, and these places are planned to maximize the flow of traffic.

Management usually makes sure there's just the right kind of retail mix; you won't be up against too many other similar boutiques, but there will be enough to draw your customer in. The shopping center will do a certain amount of advertising and promotion of its own, and they provide parking and security.

The downside, other than the high cost of rent, is that you have to play by their rules and abide by their opening hours. "I choose not to open up our stores in malls because of the high rents and the long hours of opening. Our staff drive the business, and I don't want the long mall hours to burn them out. Shorter hours mean that we can keep a smaller, more knowledgeable sales force," says Sue. She's chosen to have her boutiques in highly visible locations on streets with a lot of automobile traffic instead.

Perhaps the biggest drawback is that increasing numbers of malls seem to favor the established chain stores with their enviable brand awareness. Sometimes it's easy for an independent shop to get overlooked in the customers' mad rush to get to Banana Republic or Bebe.

Sometimes you have to pay maintenance fees in addition to the rent. It's also a bit more difficult to put a truly individual stamp on the look of your store. The nature of shopping centers is that building materials are uniform, and while store design can get the customer's attention, you couldn't manage to make your shop look like an old general store, for example.

# Strip Malls

The strip mall is the long mall with parking stalls in front, but no common interior. Each business has its own front door onto the parking lot, and usually a back door loading bay as well. The management doesn't offer security or promotions the way a true shopping center does, but then again their rents aren't nearly as high.

Generally speaking you tend not to see a lot of fashion boutiques in strip malls. They seem better suited to dollar stores and convenience stores, cafés, pizza delivery places, insurance agents and florists. This is probably due to a general lack of ambiance. The strip of parking places means that the buildings are set back from the main street, so you get less foot traffic walking past your front door. People are less likely to discover you by accident, so it would become far more important to promote your business through advertising or to make sure that your neighbors are the kind of businesses that will draw customers to the complex.

The majority of these places don't tend to exude charm, but I'm sure there are exceptions to the rule. If you found a nicely designed strip mall in a good part of town with high traffic, it might be a good bet.

## City Centers & Secondary Districts

The city center attracts a lot of people. People work there and shop on their lunch hours and after work. Other people come into the city for a day's outing of shopping, dinner or theater. They come not only from outlying neighborhoods but smaller nearby towns as well. You'll have access to a lot of customers in the heart of a city. On the flip side, rents can be astronomical, and some city centers also die down at night when the offices close and everyone goes home to the suburbs.

A secondary business district is a still-bustling, vibrant neighborhood that offers a good mix of other retail, restaurants and entertainment. Rents won't be cheap but they'll be far less than right downtown. Parking might be more convenient for your customers too.

## Retail Villages

What I call a "retail village" is planned, like a shopping center, but it is outdoors. They have a certain authentic beauty because many of the shops are older buildings with a sense of history. Often the street is landscaped with flowering trees or plants in containers and the occasional bench for weary pedestrians. There is usually an overriding aesthetic to the street, and a real estate management company ensures that all businesses complement each other and fit into the overall plan.

A common place to find a newer retail village is within the larger urban village development that has been gaining in popularity over recent years. These often consist of apartment and townhouse buildings with retail and restaurant businesses built into the ground floor. Apartment dwellers can ride the elevator downstairs and grab a coffee or do some shopping, without leaving the block they live on.

## Residential Retail Clusters

A final option would be a business cluster near a residential neighborhood. These are usually small, intimate areas with cafés and restaurants and a few retail shops. The result might be a lingerie shop nestled between a hardware store and a dentist's office.

In my own neighborhood there's a very girly boutique offering suede bikinis and feather boas in the same block as a store that sells raw chicken parts, a liquor store and a produce market. If you choose to open up here, consider the residential quality. Because most of your customers will come from the neighborhood itself, knowing your local demographic is even more important.

If it's the right neighborhood and the right block a boutique can do quite well (like my girly boutique). The rents are more affordable than they would be in a better planned area, but there's virtually nothing in the way of community promotion or security, and parking is often "potluck."

In a mixed retail environment, the specific position of the location is also important. You'll get more walk-by traffic on a main thoroughfare than if you're half a block down a side-street adjacent to that main thoroughfare. The exception here is if you're on a corner, which can be an excellent position, especially if you have windows both on the main street and the secondary street.

You'll also want to consider your neighbors. Even within the same block there can be a more desirable end and a less desirable end. It might be to your disadvantage to situate your boutique next to a bar or liquor store, or any business likely to attract a lot of panhandlers. Aggressive panhandling can prove intimidating to some customers and might keep them from approaching your store.

If there's a greasy spoon next door, you'll need to look into the ventilation system. Inhale deeply. Fried onions can smell fantastic, but do you want that kind of aroma clinging to your silk shirts and wool sweaters? Some buildings are constructed in such a way that you can never keep your neighbor's smells from entering your premises.

Food isn't the only concern here. Some of the botanical cosmetics stores and aromatherapy places, while pleasant enough, can be overpowering to the point of interfering with the neighboring businesses.

You should also check out where deliveries can be made in this type of neighborhood, which won't necessarily have a back alley access or similar. Make sure trucks will be able to get into your space to deliver your orders.

## How You Fit into the Mix

Combined with your niche, location is the most important decision you can make about your retail business. You also have to consider your niche and location together, and make sure that one complements the other.

You want to make sure there will be a good strong client base located near your store wanting to buy your product. You want to be unique enough to give customers a reason to visit your shop, but you also want to fit in with the rest of the neighborhood. It would be best if the other shops weren't in direct competition with you but were doing a good job at bringing your type of customer onto the block.

A children's wear store could do very well located near a daycare center, toy store, children's bookstore, or an elementary school where parents are coming to pick up their kids. If there's a major sporting goods or golf store on the block you might consider offering casual men's wear. And a wedding boutique might thrive near a jewelry store where a lot of brides-to-be are choosing their rings.

A community might not be the right one to support your business concept, which means that either your location or your niche will have to change.

For example, if your boutique is:

- …in the heart of a business district, you probably don't want to open a trendy teen boutique. That might do better a block from a high school.

- …in a mill town where almost everyone has a blue-collar job, you probably won't sell much business attire or evening wear at all.

- …to focus on genuine leather and fur garments, you don't want a space that's half a block from a vegetarian restaurant and across the street from an organic grocer!

A community offers more than walk-by clients, it also offers a support network and a potential source of referral business. While that close network is especially evident in a small town or village, it can be replicated to an extent even in a larger city. It means choosing to support other small businesses in the hope that they will support yours.

It means stopping in for coffee at independently owned cafés and bakeries, buying your groceries at independent markets rather than the gigantic chain supermarkets, and supporting the small, locally owned business whenever you possibly can. Get into the habit of chatting with these business owners and telling them about your shop.

"I'm so lucky to have my business in this town. We all support each other; I have lunch in the sushi restaurant next door and then the proprietor comes into my shop to find a new outfit. This community is full of good karma," boutique owner Beverly told us.

## 4.1.3   The Local Traffic

Once you've selected a few possible neighborhoods or have your eye on appropriate spaces that are for lease, you're going to want to start doing some detective work. You're going to lurk and linger and watch what goes on at various times of day and on different days of the week.

"I researched the neighborhood for five months before committing!" says Margaret. "I visited it often, in all kinds of weather. I watched in January and February, and I saw that those months were very slow. I knew I would need enough savings to see me through the first months of the year."

## Counting Customers

Find an outdoor table at a café and arm yourself with a jumbo coffee and a notebook. For each neighborhood you are considering, study the types and numbers of pedestrians that walk past. If it's an especially busy street, you might want one of those mechanical counting gadgets where your finger will click a button for each person you count.

Analyze them as best you can from a distance to find out how many potential clients pass by the businesses on a given day. This means that if you're opening a teen boutique, you probably don't count the senior citizens or the young mothers with small children. If you're opening a women's shoe store, you don't count the men. Consider the way they're dressed, the kind of shopping bags they're carrying, and whether they're equipped with briefcases or backpacks to guess if they would become a customer.

You want a reasonably accurate count of the people who are likely to walk in through your boutique's front door if it were already open for business. Of course you're only going to arrive at an educated guess; not every teenager you count is going to shop in your teen boutique, but that senior citizen might pop in and buy something for her granddaughter.

For each area you're considering, spend an hour a day for a few days counting customers. Don't make it too soon after the shops open, or too close to their closing time. Don't always choose the peak period, either. In fact, try not to count during the exact same hour every day, but mix it up a bit so you end up with a more rounded indication of street traffic for that area.

Some landlords will be able to give you numbers for walk-by traffic. That's because in high-profile shopping areas these numbers relate directly to the rent a landlord can demand. Famous streets like Madison Avenue and Melrose Avenue, Robson Street and Yonge Street have amazingly high rents that in theory are justified by the walk-by traffic that you'll have access to just by being there. Consider also whether these traffic figures reflect your chosen market.

Foot traffic is important because it represents what the neighborhood will deliver to your door, more or less by accident. However, it doesn't mean that your clientele is limited to this number, because your efforts to promote yourself will bring customers from other locations to see your boutique and what it has to offer.

## Analyzing the Results

Obviously, the higher the foot traffic numbers, the better. But it's also important to consider what your competition will be like in the area. You might be up against a lot of designer-brand stores who already have a lot of advertising muscle on their side.

Think about the hours you'd be open if you were on that street. If you'd be open from 10 a.m. to 6 p.m. on a Tuesday and during one hour you counted fifty likely customers, that would give you about 400 customers a day. Add each weekday up until you know how many customers in an average week that street would bring past your door.

Then do the same with the other neighborhoods on your shortlist. Compare the results, and give extra points to a neighborhood where rent is about the same price but the number of potential customers who walk by in given week is 10% to 50% higher.

Eliminate any locations that don't seem likely to serve your niche market, or any niche that doesn't seem appropriate to the locations you have in mind. Eventually you will arrive at the ideal combination of the neighborhood and niche; a location that is likely to be full of customers who will want the product you choose to offer. "You might get a really good deal on an out-of-the-way location without much foot traffic, but it won't be easy to let people know how to find you. You'll be better off spending a little more on a street that's well-established for retail," advises Wendy.

If you choose to lease in a mall, think about your specific location and the neighboring businesses. Are you in the main corridor of the shopping center, or down a side wing? If it's the latter, do your own customer count. How much walk-by traffic makes its way down that arm of the building, compared to the main part of the mall?

A lower number isn't necessarily a big problem, if you'll share that quieter wing with exactly the right kinds of stores that will bring the right type of customer to your door. The specific type of traffic flow is always a more important consideration than the overall traffic volume. Therefore a relatively quiet corridor with other shops that attract your customer could be a wiser choice than a busier, more expensive location with a throng of traffic that doesn't represent your market.

## 4.1.4   Evaluating a Space

As you view different spaces for your boutique, you'll begin to develop an instinct for knowing what feels right immediately. The most important influence will be things that can't be changed or would be expensive to change, such as overall square footage, and good windows for displaying product. The other things, like fitting rooms and stock rooms, can always be adapted to suit your needs and budget.

You can read through the list below to learn about different criteria you'll want to evaluate for each potential space, and then you can use the checklist at the end of the section to photocopy and take with you when you look at each space.

### Square Footage

Once you know you like the neighborhood, the next question you'll probably ask regarding any potential space is what the square footage is. A boutique by definition doesn't have to be very big. In fact, 1000 to 1200 square feet is a very common size, and depending what you're selling and how that space is organized, you might get away with only 600. More square footage is not always a good thing, since you will have to pay to maintain that additional space.

### Entrance

As a general rule, the entrance should be generous and welcoming. The front door itself should be in proportion to the size of the shop. As part of your storefront it contributes to the overall impression that beckons a customer inside.

If your store is older and/or tiny, a single width door might be sufficient for customers both coming and going. If your boutique is in a new development or a shopping center you'll probably have double-wide doors that slide apart or get propped open during business hours.

TIP: If your doors are glass make sure they're cleaned regularly, removing greasy fingerprints daily.

Some corner location boutiques have entrances on two sides. This can be to your advantage, although it's less important than having windows on two sides. Every entrance is also an exit, and sadly that means an opportunity for shoplifters. Therefore you want to make sure that all exits are visible to your staff at all times, ideally from the cash desk in the event that you're understaffed.

If there's any kind of raised threshold or some kind of obstacle that someone could trip over, consider redesigning the entrance. A sign advising people to watch their step can be distracting and sometimes tacky, and it's better not to run the risk of anyone hurting themselves.

If your shop is up (or down) a flight of stairs you'll almost certainly get a break on the rent, but give this serious thought before you commit. You'll get a lot more of your walk-by traffic actually entering your boutique door if that door is at street level. Even one short flight of stairs can be a deterrent to a busy shopper or uncommitted browser.

## Windows

The more window space you can work into your boutique, the better. Large windows allow for attractive displays that will catch your potential customer's attention, turning passersby into paying customers. A corner location allows for windows on both sides and maximizes the promotional aspect of your display space.

Most boutique windows are slightly above street level for maximum impact. They are sometimes closed in at the back, so the passerby sees a backdrop behind the window display, but cannot see into the store itself.

This puts more emphasis on the window display and doesn't allow it to get confused with interior displays or with the traffic inside the store.

A backless window that allows people to see inside your store can have its advantages as well, depending on the layout of your merchandise and your other displays.

## Lighting

Lighting is one of those interior design aspects that is a mystery to most people. When it's good we take it for granted; we only notice it when it's awful, like those horrible fluorescent tubes so common in office buildings that make everyone look as if they're suffering from a bad case of the flu. In our homes, we might notice inadequate kitchen lighting or reading lamps that aren't sufficient.

In retail shops, the problem is rarely that lighting is too dim. Sometimes it's too bright, but more often it's the wrong color or in the wrong position. You'll probably want different types of lighting for different areas of your store, such as windows, fitting rooms, cash desk, etc.

Good lighting is essential to the success of your store. It isn't just a utility; it's a selling tool that will highlight the areas you want customers to notice, like display fixtures and cases. To avoid ending up illuminating the floor or your customers, we strongly suggest consulting an interior designer or lighting technician, or learn as much as possible about it yourself. You can read a free eight-page brochure online about lighting a small retail space at **www.designlights.org/downloads/retail_ guide. pdf**.

The _Budget Guide to Retail Store Planning & Design_, by Jeff Grant, who owns a retail design consulting firm, also covers the basics of retail store design, including a chapter devoted to lighting.

## Flooring

You're looking for an attractive floor that will suit the rest of your store design. You'll want good value, something that will endure frequent traffic and will require minimal maintenance. It should be simple to install if you are putting it in yourself, easy to clean, and safe to walk on.

Since you and your staff will be standing on it for several hours a day, you'll also want something comfortable. I know people who have found concrete floors very hard on the legs and back after a few years of working in that environment, so although concrete is currently fashionable and easy to maintain, you might be better off considering another material, or at least providing some cushioning mats behind the cash desk.

Studies have shown that shoppers spend more time looking at merchandise when they're doing so in a comfortable, carpeted area. If possible, keep your merchandise on carpeted areas, but use tile "paths" between these areas to lead shoppers to your merchandise.

The _Budget Guide to Retail Store Planning & Design_, mentioned earlier, also has a chapter with advice about floor-coverings for retail stores.

## Walls and Ceilings

The majority of boutiques have painted plaster or drywall walls, which provide a clean, uncomplicated backdrop to display fixtures and racks of colorful clothing. Sometimes one or more walls will be done in mirror, brick, stone, wood, fabric, paper or glass, but it's rare to have an entire store done with one of these more costly materials.

Ceilings are somewhat more basic, although high ceilings are usually an asset. Acoustic tile is a popular option and there are many varieties of plastics that function well in a boutique. If you will be choosing a ceiling material and installing it, consult your designer for a combination of lighting and ceiling that will provide the best effect.

## Fitting Rooms

We recommend at least two to three fitting rooms for a space of 1000 to 1200 square feet, unless your product range is shoes or accessories only. These can be simple rooms with partial walls, as long as they're tall enough to give even a basketball player privacy.

Hinged doors are a nice upscale feature, but even high-end boutiques still get away with a nice fabric curtain, provided it's not so skimpy that it leaves peak-a-boo gaps at the ends. It's thoughtful to have several hooks inside, not only so your customers can hang the merchandise up, but their own clothes and handbags as well. You might want to provide a little chair or a stool for resting or balance, or for a patient child.

We suggest that you include a full-length mirror so clients don't have to wander into the larger store to view the outfit. Some boutiques deliberately exclude this feature so that the customer is forced to show sales staff how they look in the outfit, which gives the staff a chance to check them out, or offer another style or size. While this may work in some types of boutiques, it won't work in every atmosphere. Customers may get annoyed by such tactics and if so, chances are they'll just stop coming into your shop altogether.

## Staff Areas and Storeroom

You'll need a washroom for yourself and your staff, and it's a good, courteous detail to provide one that will be suitable for the occasional customer to use as well, especially if you're in the business of retailing children's wear or maternity clothing. The natural location for this would be in the back of the store, near the fitting rooms or as part of the staff room/storeroom.

The small room at the back can be called the backroom, staffroom or storeroom. It usually doubles as a staff lunch area, sometimes with a microwave, kettle or coffee maker. This room may also double as the owner's and manager's office for writing up orders, working on the staff schedule or doing other paperwork.

It is also typically used to receive new stock and store things like shoes. Often there's a back door that is kept locked and not accessed by the public; this usually leads into a loading dock or back lane where trucks can pull in when they have a delivery for you. Normally there's a buzzer for them to ring so you can come and open the door.

## Fixtures

Depending on your product, you'll require a mix of shelves, racks for hanging clothing, and perhaps a low table or two. You'll also want a cash desk and you might want one or two other display counters or racks for displaying accessories. These things needn't cost a lot, and can often be purchased secondhand. They should be sturdy but easy to move, and the position of shelves and racks should be adjustable.

You can use a graph-paper sketch of the space to draw in the particulars, such as: women's scarves (wooden rack), sales desk (60" x 45"), winter jackets, and so on. This will provide you not only with a visual, but a real sense of what will and won't work.

If there are two things that most retailers agree on in regards to layout, they are that the layout should provide customers with the ability to scan the entire store from the entrance (i.e. the forest should not block the view of the trees), and that all items should be accessible and available for customers to handle.

You might need a few mannequins or dress-forms. Mannequins should be easy to get apart and their limbs should be easy to dress in trouser legs and shirt sleeves. Don't leave your staff struggling with mannequins in store windows for hours trying to get an awkwardly bent arm into a fitted sleeve, to the amusement of passersby.

You can choose to have a custom-made cash desk if it's important that you get exactly what you want, but if you're watching your budget you should be able to get a used one that will suit your needs. You want it to be big enough to let you fold and wrap the customer's purchases and of course it also has to accommodate whatever point-of-sale system or cash register you choose.

The cash desk can be horseshoe-shaped, L- or U-shaped, but most often in a small boutique a single-sided desk will be enough. Under the counter should be storage for the receipt and journal rolls required for your printer, bags, gift boxes and wrapping tissue. Also, never situate your cash desk in an area where a line-up will block customers from getting to the merchandise.

The following are sources for retail fixtures, and you can also search your local Yellow Pages, or the trade publications listed at the end of this guide.

- *Allen Display*
  **www.allendisplay.com**

- *Robert H. Ham Store Fixtures*
  **www.robertham.com**

- *Gershel Bros. New & Used Store Fixtures*
  **www.gershelbros.com**

## Utilities

Your boutique will need modern phone lines that are adequate for credit card payments and faxes, as well as standard phone usage. (Imagine how unprofessional it would be if you couldn't ring in a customer's credit card purchase because the phone line was already in use while your employee spoke to another customer.)

You'll also probably want Internet access, lots of power outlets in convenient locations, running water in the bathroom, and depending on the climate of your location, heat and/or air conditioning. In a newer building a lot of this will already be in place, so you'll just have to check the locations of outlets and phone cables and make sure they'll be within reach of your equipment.

## Staff and Customer Parking

If they don't already live or work in the neighborhood, will people be able to get to your shop? Is there adequate parking in the neighborhood? Is it on a public transit route?

You're not required to provide parking for your staff and you might not be in a position to. If you're near a transit route, they (and you) might choose to take the bus or train, or walk if you're close enough.

The problem, of course, is that having a car can be convenient and time-efficient if you have errands to do during the daytime. On busy days, if you need to drive, you should have a plan for parking nearby. When you're preparing to sign your lease, do a little scouting around to see if you can find an inexpensive parking lot close to your location. This will be good news for you as well as for your customers.

If you're part of a strip mall, your boutique might have been assigned a couple of stalls. You don't want all of these used by staff, though; you want to leave some assigned parking for your customers. It will probably be better for you to pay to park in a nearby lot.

# Boutique Location Checklist

Use this checklist to record your impressions of different locations you are considering for your boutique.

If any of these criteria are still to be developed, note what the potential is instead.

**Square Footage**

_____

_____

_____

_____

**Entrance**

_____

_____

_____

_____

**Windows**

_____

_____

_____

_____

**Lighting**

_____

_____

_____

_____

**Flooring**

_____

_____

_____

_____

**Walls and Ceilings**

_____
_____
_____
_____

**Fitting Rooms**

_____
_____
_____
_____

**Staff Areas and Storeroom**

_____
_____
_____
_____

**Fixtures**

_____
_____
_____
_____

**Utilities**

_____
_____
_____
_____

**Staff and Customer Parking**

_____
_____
_____
_____

**Other**

_____
_____
_____
_____

# 4.2   Sources of Inventory

There are a number of ways to fill your store with product. If you choose to sell new merchandise, you can either buy it domestically or import it from another country. If you choose to buy inventory from within your own country, your freight costs will be minimal and you won't have to pay any import duties or additional taxes.

If you opt to open a secondhand store, most of your stock will come in on a consignment basis. Or if you're handy and creative, you can certainly design and manufacture items yourself. We'll look at just what each of these choices will mean in this section.

## 4.2.1   Local Designers

Supporting local fashion designers who might not have a high profile yet is often an affordable way to get product into your store. Some of your customers might consider wearing locally designed product a rewarding way to support the community, as well.

To find local designers, try:

- Asking local garment manufacturers or wholesale fabric suppliers for contacts they are working with. The Yellow Pages for a city will normally list wholesalers, manufacturers and agents under the "Clothing" section, if any exist for that area.

- Asking a fashion design school in the area if they could recommend any past students who are now working in fashion design. Their graduation ceremonies usually feature a fashion show that's open to the public, which would provide a good opportunity for you to scope out the local up-and-coming talent.

Remember that designers are creative people with their own strong vision, so unless you hire someone to create a line specifically for you, you won't be able to dictate what to make. Hiring a designer to work for your store is a great way to guarantee a constant source of fresh stock, but it's likely the designer will want you to cover their costs up front, long before you collect any revenues from sales to your customer. If you don't have that kind of money to throw around early on, you'll be better off working with a designer whose aesthetic you admire, and placing orders from their seasonal collection.

## 4.2.2   Showrooms and Show Marts

If your search for local vendors comes up empty, or if you really want the cachet of carrying widely recognized brands, you'll probably visit designers' showrooms, or meet with sales agents in a show mart. Many designers will have agents set up in the garment district or fashion markets of major fashion centers.

In the U.S., the major centers are New York, Los Angeles, Miami and Dallas, although other large cities such as Atlanta, Chicago, Denver and San Francisco will also have resources for the fashion buyer. In Canada you'll want to visit Montreal, Toronto and Vancouver.

A showroom is an office or section of an office where a manufacturer, distributor or agent displays garment samples for a buyer to examine and handle. Often the buyer places the order right there in the showroom, although other times you simply view the line, then take the order sheet, pricelist and catalog away to fax or mail it in later.

A show mart (or "mart") is a larger building that houses several agency showrooms within its walls. It's sort of like the wholesale equivalent of a big shopping mall with many individual boutiques inside. These buildings are only open to people in the trade, and ID is required just to get in. You can contact the major North American marts listed below directly to find out about upcoming events.

### Atlanta Apparel Mart

*Website:*   **www.americasmart.com**

*Address:*   240 Peachtree Street N.W., Suite 2200
Atlanta, GA 30303-1327

*Phone:*   (404) 220-3000

### Dallas Market Center

*Website:*   **www.dallasmarketcenter.com**

*Address:*   2100 Stemmons Freeway
Dallas, TX 75207

*Phone:*   (214) 655-6100 or 1-800-DAL-MKTS

## Denver Merchandise Mart

*Website:*   **www.denvermart.com**

*Address:*   451 East 58th Avenue, Ste. #4270
Denver, CO 80216-8470

*Phone:*   (303) 292-6278 or 1-800-289-6278

## California Market Center (LA)

*Website:*   **www.californiamarketcenter.com**

*Address:*   110 East 9th Street, Ste. #A727
Los Angeles, CA 90079

*Phone:*   (213) 630-3600 or 1-800-225-6278

## Miami International Merchandise Mart

*Website:*   **www.miamimart.net/index.asp**

*Address:*   777 NW. 72 Ave.
Miami, FL 33126

*Phone:*   (305) 261-2900 Ext. 135

## The Fashion Center (NY)

*Website:*   **www.fashioncenter.com**

*Address:*   209 West 38th Street
New York, NY 10018

*Phone:*   (212) 764-9600

## Montreal Apparel Mart

*Website:*   **www.555chabanel.com/index.aspx?LANG=EN-CA**

*Address:*   555 Chabanel Street West, Suite 1508
Montreal, P.Q. H2N 2J2

*Phone:*   (514) 381-5921

If you find that the major cities near you don't have much in the way of fashion resources, you should consider traveling to one that does, preferably during a fashion or market week, or at least in the spring and fall.

# Buying Wholesale

Unless your boutique deals entirely in clothes by local designers, or you design and sell your own products, much of your sales merchandise will be bought from wholesalers. The wholesale concept is simple: wholesalers buy "close to the source" and purchase large quantities, reducing the per-unit price. They in turn resell the product at a profit to retailers, but for prices below what the retailer will charge.

Your wholesale buying will generally take place at apparel marts or trade shows. To be permitted to make wholesale purchases you will need proof that you are a business owner or working on behalf of a retail store: a valid business license, and/or proof that you're licensed to resell items, such as a tax number, sales tax permit, or both. Many apparel marts will also insist that you fill out an annual registration form that provides more information about your business.

There is an etiquette to wholesale purchasing that you need to be aware of. For example, many wholesalers deal on a cash-only basis. Some will accept checks, but rarely do wholesalers accept credit cards, so leave the plastic at home. There may also be a minimum quantity you will be required to order, so ask what the minimums are in advance.

Also, keep in mind that the garments you buy from a wholesaler won't be available to take back to the boutique with you that day. Instead, you'll have to find out when the garments will be shipped, and make shipping arrangements, often at your own cost. Some wholesalers will insist that you pay COD (cash on delivery) at first, but eventually most will allow you to set up an account with them and arrange for later payment of goods.

Lastly, sales tax is not paid to the wholesaler, but don't think this means your purchases are "tax-free." You must file your purchases with the county, state, provincial and/or federal tax authorities (depending where you live) and pay them the sales tax based on the retail value of your purchases. You will recover this cost with the sales tax collected from your customers.

## 4.2.3 Fashion Trade Shows

The big fashion centers such as New York, LA and Toronto have market or fashion weeks which bring designers and buyers together, usually twice a year, at a series of trade shows. These shows usually take place in large convention and exhibition centers. They're arranged so that each vendor can set up a booth or mini-showroom with samples and swatches and order forms.

Buyers usually make an appointment in advance to view the collection at the trade show. Either an agent or a sales rep will show you the line and you will write your order then and there. The trade show normally lasts three to four days, and you can do your buying for an entire season at that time.

Trade shows are only for business people; they are not open to members of the public and most organizers will insist on proof that you're attending to buy, not one of the curious hoping to browse. Current apparel trade shows are listed by either calendar or city at:

- *Infomat: Fashion Industry Information Services and Search Engine*
  **www.infomat.com/calendar/infsd0000044.html**

- *Apparel News.net Tradeshow Calendar*
  **www.apparelnews.net/calendar**

For a schedule of upcoming shows, also see:

- *Fashion Week L.A.*
  **www.fashionweekla.com**

- *IMG Fashion Events Calendar (NY)*
  **www.imgworld.com/entertainment/fashion/**

- *Toronto Fashion Incubator*
  **www.fashionincubator.com/happenings/calendar**

You should also consider traveling to the international fashion centers of Paris, Milan, Hong Kong and London to visit their market weeks, if not necessarily to purchase, at least for inspiration.

- *Hong Kong Fashion Week Fall/Winter*
  **http://hkfashionweekfw.tdctrade.com**

- *Hong Kong Fashion Week Spring/Summer*
  **http://hkfashionweekss.tdctrade.com**

- *Camera Nazionale della Moda Italiana (Milan)*
  **www.cameramoda.it/eng/eventi/eventi.php**

- *Milano Moda Donna*
  **www.eventseye.com/fairs/trade_fair_event_1862.html**

- *London Fashion Week*
  **www.londonfashionweek.co.uk**

- *What's on When: Paris Fashion Week (Paris)*
  **www.modeaparis.com/va/collections**

## 4.2.4   Consignment Goods

When you acquire goods on consignment, you're not actually purchasing them. The things you "buy" remain the property of the person who brought them to you, until you sell them and pay him for them.

This method of getting product is most common for those setting up a secondhand or vintage clothing store. It's an excellent way to keep your overhead low and your cash flowing. You don't have to pay your suppliers until your customer has paid you.

Secondhand clothing stores can be very successful and lucrative. Don't think Salvation Army, think high-end designer boutiques in up-market neighborhoods. I can think of a few who sell only the likes of Ann Klein, Rei Kawakubo, Chanel and Versace, and they only accept garments that are in pristine condition. The retail prices are still far higher than what you'd expect to pay for a generic brand, but a mere fraction of what these designer brands would fetch the first time around.

Usually consignment will mean purchasing slightly used goods. As mentioned, you might be able to acquire brand-new product in this way, if you work with a local designer who wants to promote his line by having it featured in a retail store.

Whether it's brand new consignment or secondhand, look into your insurance policy and make sure the merchandise will be covered. After a burglary, boutique owner Wendy discovered that her policy didn't cover her merchandise because it was acquired on consignment and therefore she didn't technically "own" it.

If you're interested in going this route, the *FabJob Guide to Become a Secondhand Store Owner* is full of insider tips and valuable advice on buying and selling gently used items.

---

## Design Your Own Garments

If you have a strong sense of style and a clear vision, you might choose to further strengthen your unique brand and image by designing and manufacturing your own products, like boutique owner Jane does.

"I loved dressing my kids in vintage clothing when they were small. When I decided to start my own business, I knew I wanted to offer that sweet, old-fashioned styling. I decided to design and manufacture my own line, with the look and feel of an earlier era," she explains.

The major advantage is that no one else in the world will be able to sell exactly the same item, so if you offer a fantastic product, you will have exclusive control of it.

The main disadvantages are selling an unrecognized brand, and the additional start-up costs for purchasing fabrics, making patterns and samples, and manufacturing your own line. These things can add up and they all have to be paid for long before your customer is able to walk through your door and buy a finished dress.

In order to go this route, you'll have to learn not only about buying and retailing, but about garment designing and manufacturing, which is obviously beyond the scope of this guide. But not to worry — an excellent resource is the *FabJob Guide to Become a Fashion Designer*. It will tell you everything you need to know before you undertake designing your own line.

---

# 4.3 Buying for Your Boutique

Buying for your boutique is both an art and a science. The artist in you will determine the labels, pieces of clothing and colors that will be precisely the right mix of product to wow your customer — not today or tomorrow, but six months down the road. Then the "scientist" gets involved to determine the sizing assortment and the quantity of product, based on past sales and projections. It won't take many seasons of business before you have a real feel for what your customers like and what will sell quickly.

## 4.3.1 How Much to Start With

Deciding how much opening inventory you need will, by necessity, involve a bit of guesswork. A safe rule of thumb is to start small. You'll rely on the figures you came up with in your business plan that reflect the size and scope of your boutique to determine what "small" means to you.

Your budget will detail what you are open to buy (OTB) for a given time period. Let's say your budget for the year's first quarter was $30,000, but it's February 1 and you have already placed orders for $25,000. Your OTB for the rest of February and March is therefore $5,000, and you'll need to stick to that.

You can work backwards from anticipated sales, as Sue explains: "Let's say that for your first year you expect to do $120,000-$200,000 in sales. You can probably open with a third of that inventory, and turn your stock over three times in the year. I'd suggest opening with about $40,000 retail value, which is going to be $15,000 to $20,000 cost of goods, depending on your markup."

How quickly a given product sells after it is received in your shop is called "sell-through." If the little black dresses from In-Wear have all sold out two weeks after they were put on your selling floor, then that indicates excellent sell-through. If all six of the lemon-yellow jumpsuits are still hanging around your boutique three months after they arrived, the sell-through is awful.

You don't want to start off with too much inventory that ties up your cash flow and sells slowly. It's much better to start with a little, notice that it's selling fast and at full price, and then replenish your stock. This way allows for a lot more flexibility as you learn what your customer tends to like.

Also, the more expensive your niche and product, the less quantity of stock you need to buy. Margaret started her boutique with 150 pieces of clothing, accessories and artwork. Most of the clothing was two-piece dresses and coordinating separates. She put about half of them on dress forms (which gives the boutique an exclusive, uncluttered look and shows the clothing off to its best advantage). The remaining items hang on a single rack at the back.

Imagine the stores you like to go into on a regular basis. Chances are that the less-expensive stores are packed with a lot more merchandise than the higher-end shops. The hangers are closer together and sometimes fight for space on the rack to the point where garments are constantly being pushed off the rack. If your niche is high-end, keep your store appearance clean and minimalist.

Wendy cautions against being too minimalist, though. "Customers like to have options; it makes their shopping experience more entertaining." Conflicting advice? Not necessarily. It depends on your market, your target customer's shopping habits, and your average price point. Just make sure your inventory reflects who you are.

You can also take advantage of any contacts you have in the boutique industry (your mentors, suppliers, manufacturers, designers, etc.) to help you plan your start-up stock levels, as well as place orders later on. Margaret has such a good relationship with one of her suppliers that she often buys product sight unseen. Knowing the designer's style and quality standards, she trusts her tastes and understanding of Margaret's market. She'll give her a budget and ask the designer to choose a few things that will be suitable for the store. She's never been disappointed yet.

## 4.3.2   Selection Criteria

While you will want most of your selection to be the kinds of things you like yourself (after all, genuine enthusiasm for your product will make it easier to sell), your customers' tastes will take priority when you buy for your boutique.

"Follow your instincts that tell you what other people are going to like. This means occasionally putting personal preferences aside," confides Sue. So if you wouldn't wear an earth tone to your own funeral, remember that a certain proportion of your customer base is going to feel most comfortable in browns, beiges and greens.

Even if you place an order for an item that you decide is awful once it arrives in your store, there's still hope. A visual merchandising teacher of mine once said that if you decide that you hate something you or your partner bought, put it in the window and it'll sell in a snap. I found myself following his suggestion on a few occasions as a retail manager, and the man was right. There's no accounting for tastes! Here are some of the criteria that will affect how you select your stock.

## Fashion Forecasting

Remember that you're going to have to stay six months ahead of the styles. The fashions you see in a designer showroom or a trade show booth might appear outlandish or laughable, but if that designer has done his homework, the trendsetters will be quick to scoop them up, and the masses will soon follow.

If you aren't too sure of your own instincts, or are planning on retailing high-end fashions, you can always consult with a trend forecasting service, as many fashion designers do when developing garments. Trend forecasters put out various publications that go into the details of garment styling, fabrications, accessories and colors that are likely to take off. Trend forecasting service providers (like Doneger Creative Services at **www.doneger.com/web/231.htm**) also often attend the major trade shows.

# Discounted Product

Most boutiques sell clothing that is known as "ready to wear". These are garments mass-produced for the public and sold on racks, as opposed to "couture", which is custom-made for the client who walks in the shop's door. Within the ready to wear category, there are some varieties of clothing that will cost you less to stock, because they are damaged or imitation. Here is a look at what your options are.

### "Knock offs"

This describes the practice of a lower-end manufacturer directly copying the design, fabrication, and sometimes even logo to make a very similar, inexpensively priced product for the mass market.

The knock off is a tricky concept to categorize, and whether or not you choose to sell them is up to how you feel about it. In its purest and most deplorable form it imitates every detail of the original design: the cut, fabric, color, trims, etc. This is devoid of creativity and seems unfair to the inspiration of the original designers.

Yet many designers, even some prestigious fashionistas, resort to copying another design at one time or another. The question is one of degree; how much of the original is directly copied and how much of the resulting garment is changed to reflect the individual's contribution.

### "Seconds"

This is merchandise in less than perfect condition, often reduced and sold "as is" with the understanding that it cannot be returned. Also called factory seconds if the defect is a result of manufacturing; some discount outlets do a good job selling designer's factory seconds and often showroom samples to the public at much lower prices than the first (or perfect) condition product would cost. The label is often cut or removed from the garment because the designer doesn't really want his or her name associated with the imperfect product.

Selling designer factory seconds, samples and out-of-season closeouts might be an idea for your niche if you have access to a market who likes to dress fashionably on a lean budget.

## Product Ratios

Deciding how much of each item to buy requires a thoughtful study of your market. Most of the time you won't be selling the same number of dresses as coats, or even a similar ratio of tops to bottoms. For the product mix, you'll want to model your store after an average wardrobe. Most wardrobes, and therefore most stores, will consist largely of "separates", which are tops and bottoms sold separately.

> **TIP:** Most experts recommend more tops than bottoms, and a suggested ratio of three to two is not uncommon. This makes sense when you think about it; tops tend to get washed more frequently and therefore wear faster!

A women's store will generally include a few dresses as well, and men's dressy or career stores might have a selection of suits. Both will have smaller numbers of things like coats and jackets. The exception of course, is specialty shops like jean stores, whose primary focus is on pants. They'll have fewer, if any, coordinating shirts, blouses and sweaters. It's less common to see a store that just sells tops, unless it's a novelty T-shirt shop.

One good way to find the right formula for mixing product is to go into an established shop that you hope to model yours after. Try to go early in the season, like February for spring or August for fall, when they'll have received a lot of product but won't be sold out yet.

Walk through the store as if you were a shopper, but count the numbers of styles they're offering in tops, bottoms, dresses or suits, coats etc. Once you do this in a few shops, it should give you a pretty good idea of the ratio you're looking for. You might also consult a wardrobe planning book for ideas on ratios and accessories, such as _Looking Good: A Comprehensive Guide to Wardrobe Planning, Color, & Personal Style Development_, by Nancy Nix-Rice and Pati Palmer, or the _Chic Simple_ series for men and women, by Kim Johnson Gross and Jeff Stone.

Julie Culshaw, owner of Timmel Fabrics, has a website that sells fabrics and other sewing supplies for those who like to sew their own wardrobes. Her article, "Sewing with a Plan" (**www.timmelfabrics.com/ wardrobe.htm**) has solid advice that even those who are hopeless with needle and thread will find compelling.

## Strategic Size Mix

The size mix is going to vary according to your location, your demographic and your niche, but chances are you will not be ordering the same proportion of extra-smalls or extra-larges to mediums. Study your market, consider their size and shape, and buy accordingly.

In women's wear, you'll sell more mediums than any other size, unless your market happens to be younger women, or the local build is very slight. For men's wear, the highest proportion of sales is more likely to be in the large category. In fact, some lines actually start at medium for men and don't bother with a small unless they're catering to young men and teens. The most common shirt sizes for men are 15 1/2-16" necks, and trousers sell most in the 34-36" waist size.

Children's wear is trickier because the sizing relates to their ages; you'll have to think about the position of the baby boom in your area. You might have more 2- and 3-year-olds locally, or you might have more that fall into the 6 to 8 bracket. The demographic information explained in section 4.1.1 will help you out here.

Often the sales agent or rep you do your buying with will be able to give you some advice based on the sizes they most commonly sell for that product range or label. If you are totally uncomfortable with the prospect of choosing a mix of clothing, you might choose to work with a professional buyer.

This doesn't have to be someone you hire on a full-time basis; you can find someone who will work on a consulting basis. One of the major trade shows is probably the best place to find a professional buyer; or you could inquire with the manufacturer's sales agents.

## Deep or Wide Buying

The number of units you buy in a given style is known as how "deep" you buy. A buyer who chooses ten styles of blouse but only one piece in each size is buying "wide." A buyer who spends the same budget on one style but orders ten in each size is buying very "deep."

Margaret is an example of someone who chooses to buy wide. She typically buys only one or two pieces of each style. That way she's offering her customer something truly unique and exclusive. If you buy a royal blue silk coat and choose only one piece each in small, medium and large, your customer will know that she's unlikely to run into people with the same jacket everywhere she goes. She'll feel that what she's buying is more special.

Some suppliers, distributors or agents will accuse you of "cherry-picking" their line if you don't commit to a certain level of representing their product. They might not allow you to buy, say, 1 sweater style in 3 different sizes. The bigger, higher-profile designers might even insist that if you're going to be one of their vendors you represent a reasonable selection of any given collection. There's a point to be made here; you can give greater presence to their look if you have more pieces to show. It will also be easier to merchandise your store by designer if you have a good solid range of styles that were intended to work together.

## 4.3.3   Placing Orders

When you view a vendor's collection, whether in their permanent showroom or in a temporary booth set up at a trade show, you'll often want to make the best use of your time by writing your order then and there. Most often they'll have an order form for you to use. These usually come pre-printed with style numbers, descriptions, wholesale prices, colors and size selections. You will find a sample order form on the next page.

## Ordering Tips

After you place your order, most vendors will send you an order confirmation, acknowledging that they have received your order and will be making plans to produce the pieces you requested. You should check this carefully to make sure that the styles, colors, sizes and quantities

# Sample Order Form

## Fall/Winter 2008 Collection Order Form

| Retailer: | | Date order received: | |
| Contact: | | Updates: | |
| Ship to: | | Start ship: | |
| | | In store: | |
| Phone: | | *Ship dates are estimates, dates are not confirmed at this time | |
| Fax: | | Terms: | |
| Email: | | Credit card #: | |
| Bill to (if different from ship to): | | Exp. date: | |
| | | Check #: | |
| Instructions: | | | |
| Ship via: | | | |

| Style # | Style Name | Color | Sizes | | | | | | | Total Units | Suggested Retail | Wholesale Unit Price | Total Dollars |
|---|---|---|---|---|---|---|---|---|---|---|---|---|---|
| | | | 2 | 4 | 6 | 8 | 10 | 12 | 12y | | | | |
| | | | | | | | | | | | | | |
| | | | | | | | | | | | | | |
| | | | | | | | | | | | | | |
| | | | | | | | | | | | | | |

are just what you wanted. Mistakes happen in data entry all the time and you are responsible for noting any errors.

The order confirmation will mention your payment terms, so if they want you to pre-pay for the order or pay cash on delivery (COD) you'll need to make sure that funds are available near the time of shipping. It should also give you a ship date. As that date draws near you should contact the supplier's head office to make sure they're on schedule. There are so many details in this business that delays are the norm rather than the exception.

When you place or confirm an order, you can write a "cancellation date" on it. That means you are not obligated to accept late merchandise shipped after that date. For example, if you want every piece of your order shipped by February 28, but the manufacturer runs into a problem with a fabric and cannot deliver until March 20, you do not have to accept the order.

Keep in mind that if it's a significant order your store will have less merchandise to sell and less profit to generate. Under such an unfortunate condition you might have to scramble to replace that stock by seeing if you can increase your orders from other suppliers, or evaluate if you can still accept the late shipment.

Try to arrange it so if you purchase from five vendors, not all vendors will ship your spring order on the same day. That would make a lot of unpacking and pressing for you to do, and a lot of payments to come up with all at once. There are also sales advantages to staggering your deliveries. Customers will have a greater interest and more reason for checking in if you're getting new stock every week or two.

Obviously there are a few months of the year when you don't want new product; maybe it's the end of the season and everyone's starting to slash their prices. But during the peak selling season, it will be to your advantage to get delivery at least twice a month.

## Receiving the Order

When your order is shipped, the vendor should include a packing list, which will resemble your order confirmation in a slightly different format. You must check this as you open each box and count the items inside to make sure they correspond with your packing list, and that the packing list corresponds with your order. Sometimes, for reasons beyond a supplier's control, you'll be short-shipped the odd item. However they shouldn't over-ship or substitute items without your authorization.

The packing list should also match the invoice that they send you. If the packing list reflects items that you didn't receive you should call the vendor right away and let them know about the error. Particularly if you've pre-paid you'll need to make sure they issue you a credit. If they've given you terms (meaning you'll get a bill to be paid within a specified amount of time) they'll need to correct and send you a new invoice.

It's important to check your invoices and make sure you're only paying for product actually received. Once you know they're correct it's important to pay your invoices in a timely matter and protect your credit rating. With careful credit management in your first year you should be able to negotiate for better terms with subsequent orders.

## Other Purchasing

You'll also need to buy things like hangers, gift boxes and bags, stationery, etc. for your boutique. When you order these things you can use your own purchase order and provide the supplier with instructions for such questions as where, when and how to ship your order.

On the next page, you will find a template of a fairly standard purchase order (also called a P.O.). Each P.O. you issue should have its own number that the supplier will then refer to on their packing slips and invoices. This will make your accountant's job easier when it comes time to pay the invoices; it will be easier to locate your P.O. and make sure the purchase was authorized.

You can have a bunch of purchase orders printed with your store name, address and a sequence of P.O. numbers, or you can just create a form on your computer and develop a system for making sure you don't duplicate the numbers. It's a good idea to keep a log of all P.O.s too, with the P.O. number, the date issued, total value and supplier.

# Sample Purchase Order

| Bill to: | | To: | |
|---|---|---|---|
| Company name: | | Company name: | |
| Address: | | Address: | |
| City: | | City: | |
| State: | | State: | |
| ZIP: | | ZIP: | |
| Phone: | | Phone: | |
| Fax: | | Fax: | |

| | |
|---|---|
| Purchase Order #: | |
| Date: | |
| Terms: | |
| Ship Date: | |

| Item | Qty. | Unit Cost | Extension |
|---|---|---|---|
| | | | |
| | | | |
| | | | |
| | | | |
| | | | |
| | | Subtotal | |
| | | Tax | |
| | | Total | |

| | |
|---|---|
| Freight Forwarder: | |
| Ship-to Address (if different from billing address): | |
| Purchaser Contact Info: | |

## 4.3.4   Importing From Other Countries

Importing refers to the practice of sourcing and purchasing garments or accessories that were made outside your own country. Even when you buy from an international vendor at a trade show in your own country, you are in effect "importing" the product you intend to sell.

When you import garments, you'll have to factor in additional costs to the basic price per garment, such as the cost of freight (getting your order delivered to your door), import duties and/or taxes, and fees to a customs broker. Customs brokers are government-licensed individuals, working as independents or for a brokerage firm, who work on behalf of the importer (you). You are not required to use a customs broker to import clothing, but it's a good idea if you have never dabbled in international trade before.

Customs brokers take responsibility for completing and filing the necessary paperwork, ensuring that all duties and taxes are paid, and for following through on seeing that your goods are legally cleared through customs. They can also advise on the best shipping routes and transportation options for getting your merchandise from customs to your boutique.

International trade is a complex web of rules and regulations, numerous classifications and quotas. You don't want to risk having your merchandise held in customs for weeks or months (slowly but surely going out of season and out of style) because you filled out the wrong form.

Once you decide on a broker, the first thing you'll be asked to provide is detailed information about your shipment: country of origin, type of material, etc. This information serves as the means to provide you with a quote for duties, taxes, shipping, and brokerage fees.

TIP:   The basic difference between a duty and a tax is that a duty is a levy placed on commodities, where as a tax is something that is levied on an individual. While you might avoid import duties on certain items, taxes are an inevitable part of doing business.

Every detail, down to whether or not a sweater is knit or woven, is applied to a calculation that determines how much you pay in import duties and taxes. Brokers charge a fee or flat rate based on the total value of your shipment. Many brokerages offer free online quotes.

As noted, customs brokers handle paying the duties and taxes. To do this, most brokerages operate using a client-account system. This is a line of credit that is set up with the broker or brokerage that's used to pay all duties and taxes to the appropriate agencies. You pay the broker directly, within a predetermined amount of time. Of course, establishing a brokerage account is subject to your credit approval.

One resource which may help you find a customs broker near you is Leonard's Guide Online at **www.leonardsguide.com**. Click on "Weblink," then on "Related Service Companies," then on "Customs Brokers."

## 4.3.5   Buying On Consignment

When you are opening a consignment store, word tends to spread quickly. Members of the public call you to make an appointment, usually to bring in several items, not just one or two. They will either wait while you go through them, or leave them with you to inspect.

### Being Selective

If you're taking in secondhand product, examine it with a meticulous eye for stains, burns, snags, holes and other damage. Smell it to make sure it's fresh. Your boutique should sell only first quality merchandise in excellent condition. The things that are brought to you should be cleaned, pressed and on hangers.

Beverly encourages consignment buyers to be selective. "Everyone who brings you something will insist that it's beautiful. Sometimes it really is. But don't clutter up your store with too much ho-hum. Less is definitely more; keep the racks clear so customers feel more encouraged to look through them."

Many of the vendors who bring their clothes in to sell will also become your customers, so exercise diplomacy when rejecting the things they bring in. Try to find a stain or a small hole that makes it unacceptable instead of suggesting that their style is outdated (or was never fashionable in the first place).

# Sample Boutique Consignment Agreement

This agreement is made on *[date]* between *[name of the consignment shop]*, herein referred to as "Seller", and *[individual or designer]*.

Whereas *[individual or designer]* wishes to sell *[description of item(s)]* by consigning said item(s) to *[name of consignment shop]* for sale, it is understood:

That Seller agrees to display item(s) in a prominent place in his/her establishment.

That Seller will make every attempt to obtain the best possible price for the consigned merchandise and will accept no less than $_____ as purchase price.

That for his/her efforts Seller is entitled to retain _____ % *(percent)* of the purchase price.

That should a sale be effectuated, Seller shall forward a check for the amount of the full purchase price less the aforementioned _____ % *(percent)* to Consignee within 10 days of the receipt of same.

That Seller represents that he/she maintains insurance for theft and damage, and that the consigned merchandise will be covered by said insurance while it is in his possession.

That Consignee agrees to leave the merchandise with Seller for a minimum of ___ days.

That should the merchandise remain unsold at the end of the consignment period and a decision be made by the Consignee to remove said merchandise, any costs incurred by the delivery of same to Consignee shall be borne by Consignee.

Signed on: _____ *(date)*

_____

*Consignor*

_____

*Consignee*

## A Tracking System

When you buy consignment items, you'll want to set up an account for each person who brings you goods to sell. If your supplier's name is Jane Nelson and she's the twenty-seventh supplier you have whose surname begins with N, you might give her account the number N27.

The products will normally be tagged with a selling price and an identifying number that links to that account. When you've made a list of the things you want, you'll note them in a ledger under an account number. Whatever numbering system you develop, you'll need to keep meticulous records so that you can credit the account with each sale and note the amount it sold for. Tag the garments with the selling price and the account number, then when the item is sold, you'll make a note in the specific vendor's account: "Fuchsia tweed Prada jacket. Sold for $120 on November 18. Credit account N27 for $55."

You and your supplier should agree to a retail price as well as a discount structure if the garment doesn't sell immediately. If she wants to take an item back before it gets discounted too low, that should be her right. You might also choose to set a limit on how long you'll keep trying to sell the pieces. Often consignment businesses ask suppliers whether they want to collect unsold pieces after say, three months, or donate them to a charity organization of the shop's choice.

Even three months may be a bit excessive — make sure you keep your consignment product fresh. "Usually if a secondhand piece is going to sell, it sells within the first week it's in the store," Beverly told us, based on her experience.

## 4.4   Pricing Merchandise

We're going to spend quite a bit of time on the idea of pricing merchandise. There's a bit of math involved — a few formulas, and some percentages. I apologize in advance to those of you who find this stuff more boring than looking at someone's stamp collection.

The unavoidable truth is that correct pricing is very, very important. Think about it this way: *Perfect Pricing Leads to Plump Profits.* The perfect price will take into account your indirect costs. The perfect price will ensure that your business is able to pay for all its overhead and still make a profit to be reinvested.

Pricing can make or break your business. It can fuel your success, or ensure that you go under within the first year. This isn't to scare you, but it should get your attention. If you understand pricing, profit, margins and markup, you're that much closer to running a thriving retail business.

## 4.4.1   Learning the Math

We can't make you do it, but we suggest that you make a serious attempt to learn the math involved in pricing and profitability. If percentages are a foreign language to you, then I suggest you take a crash course. You may never become fluent, but absorbing the basics will directly contribute to the profitability of your business. Let's show you why.

So, a boutique owner buys a T-shirt that costs $10. He marks up the T-shirt 100%, which means that his retail price is $20. But let's say that it doesn't sell at $20. He decides to put the T-shirt on sale at 60% off the original retail price, and it sells. That's a good thing, right?

Wrong. Do you see the problem? He sold the T-shirt for less than it cost him. And even if he had sold the T-shirt for exactly what his direct cost was, that wouldn't be enough to keep the boutique in business, because he still has to pay for rent, utilities, wages, packing materials, etc.

Don't be embarrassed if you failed to see the problem. Lots of people hate math and struggle with percentages — that's one of the reasons you might choose to hire a bookkeeper and an accountant. But it is still imperative that you have a basic understanding of pricing concepts. It doesn't have to be all in your head, either. Using a calculator or a spreadsheet program is perfectly acceptable.

For some quick and user-friendly practice with percentages, visit Retail Sales Calculator at **www.csgnetwork.com/retailsalescalc.html** (be sure to check out the Retail Margin and Markup Table link, too, which you'll find helpful after reading section 4.4.2).

## 4.4.2   Basic Pricing Concepts

The language of retail pricing uses a few terms you might not be familiar with. We're going to define them first so that the rest of this section makes sense to you. Of course this is a complex topic that could fill an entire book… and in fact, it has filled many!

Two popular selections if you would like to explore pricing concepts further are *The Strategy and Tactics of Pricing*, by Thomas T. Nagle, and *Retail Pricing Strategies and Market Power*, by Gordon Mills.

### Turnover/Sales/Revenue

Many businesses refer to turnover as the dollar value of all the items you sold in a given period. For example, if you ring $25,000 of sales through the cash register in July, then turnover for July was $25,000. The term is interchangeable with the more general term of "sales."

That said, many boutique owners use it in a different sense as well. It can also mean how often your product is bought and sold within any given period. A boutique may experience complete turnover (all products purchased and moved out of the store) a number of times a year. Maximizing turnover maximizes your profits, although it also requires cash flow to pay for the additional merchandise coming in.

> **TIP:**   Don't confuse this with staff turnover, which refers to how often employees come and go. High sales turnover is a good indication of a solid business; high staff turnover is inevitably a cash drain.

### Cost Price/Cost of Goods Sold

This is the actual cost to you for any item you are selling, and is comprised of direct and indirect costs to obtain your inventory. For example, if you buy 100 T-shirts for $1,000, then the direct cost of each T-shirt is $10. This is what you paid your vendor.

However, if you also had to pay $100 for shipping, the cost price of each T-shirt would increase by $1. On top of that, if you imported these T-shirts from Thailand, your customs duty paid might have been $200 in total. The brokerage fees and import licenses could have added up to an additional $200. The total cost to you per T-shirt would then have increased to $15 each:

| | | |
|---|---|---|
| Purchase price: | | $1,000 |
| Shipping: | + | $100 |
| Duty: | + | $200 |
| Brokerage fees: | + | $200 |
| Total cost: | = | $1,500 |
| Divided by 100 shirts: | = | $15 per shirt |

## Markup

This is the amount you "mark up" an item from its cost price to its retail price. Markup can be expressed as a dollar amount or a percentage. For example, if your cost price on a leather jacket is $200 and you decide to retail it for $500, your markup can be expressed as $300, or 150%.

| | | |
|---|---|---|
| Your cost price | | $200 |
| Markup* | + | $300 |
| Retail Price: | = | $500 |

*Difference between cost price and retail price*

To determine markup by percentage, divide markup by cost price and multiply by 100:

$$(300 \div 200) \times 100 = 150\%$$

How much you markup is of course important, but it isn't the only factor that will determine your profitability. It is part of an overall balance of the product and the turnover.

Sue mentions one favorite vendor as an example. The markup she takes on their product is only 100% instead of the 150% she takes on average, but the line is so popular with her customers that the stock she buys turns over 18-20 times a year, instead of the more usual four times a year.

The resulting sales volume makes them her most profitable vendor, despite the leaner markup.

**TIP:** When you look at computer systems make sure you research the kind of reports they'll produce. One that lists your most profitable vendors and/or styles will be of immense value when you do your buying.

Keystone markup is the practice of retailing a product for exactly twice what you paid for it, also known as 100% markup. This was once very common in apparel, but many retailers now choose to mark up product by more than that, as keystoning is not always sufficient to lead to strong profits.

Some boutique owners interviewed for this book say they now apply an average markup of 150%. "Average" means they will take a slightly lower markup on a very high-priced item, and a much higher markup on inexpensive things like accessories. Why?

A necklace that costs you $15 could sell for $30 at a $15 profit. You might decide to resell it for $35 instead, so you're making $5 more profit with each sale of a small item. Since people aren't likely to balk at paying $5 more, you still make the sale. You get a small amount more, but you get it fairly frequently. If you tried to mark up a leather coat by $50, your customer may keep shopping around for a better price, so you make sales less frequently.

## Profit

Profit can be expressed in a number of different ways. As an example, let's look at that month of July, when your turnover was $25,000. If the total direct cost of goods of all the items sold was $10,000, then your "gross profit" for July was $15,000.

| | | |
|---|---|---|
| Turnover: | | $25,000 |
| Total cost price: | - | $10,000 |
| Gross profit: | = | $15,000 |

You can determine the "net profit" by subtracting the overhead (the cost of running the boutique, such as wages, rent, utility bills, insurance, etc.). Net profit is what your business actually makes after all the costs are accounted for. Net profit will lead to a healthy business that can in part finance its own growth.

| | | |
|---|---|---|
| Gross profit: | | $15,000 |
| Overhead | - | $9,000 |
| Net profit: | = | $6,000 |

As you can see, the net profit is considerably less than the gross profit. Learning to balance turnover, gross profit and overhead so that you end up with a decent net profit will be part of the ongoing and ever-changing balancing act of running your boutique.

## Margin

Your margin is the percentage of your sales or revenue that is over and above what things cost you. Your gross margin is in relation to what your goods sold cost you, while your net margin takes into account your operating costs.

Margin and markup are often confused. Markup is expressed in relation to your total cost of goods, whereas margin is expressed as a percentage of your total sales or turnover. 100% markup means that a shirt cost you $10 and you sold it for $20, but that's only 50% gross margin.

Let's look at the same example using leather jackets.

| | | |
|---|---|---|
| Turnover*: | | $25,000 |
| Total cost price**: | - | $10,000 |
| Gross profit: | = | $15,000 |

*50 leather jackets retailed at $500 each*

**50 leather jackets with cost price of $200 each*

| | | |
|---|---|---|
| Gross profit: | | $15,000 |
| Overhead: | - | $9,000 |
| Net profit: | = | $6,000 |

To determine gross margin, divide gross profit by turnover and multiply by 100:

15,000 (GP) ÷ 25,000 (TO) x 100 = 60% gross margin

To determine net margin, divide net profit by turnover and multiply by 100:

6,000 (Net Margin) ÷ 25,000 (TO) x 100 = 24% net margin

So even though your markup was 150%, your gross margin was 60% and your net margin was only 24%.

There is a reason that understanding this concept is so important, which goes back to the example at the beginning of this section. You will sometimes need to discount items as a promotional tool, or to move slow-moving product (clearance). Clearance goods get marked down and usually stay marked down until they sell. Often that means taking further markdowns to move them from your store.

However, if you discount items more than your net margin will allow, then your boutique will be making a loss rather than a profit. Always keep in mind the operating costs that factor into the net figures.

## 4.4.3   Putting It All Together

When you understand the concepts outlined above, you will see that you should keep your overall net profit margin in mind when deciding how much to mark up your product.

For example, if you know that your monthly overhead is $9,000, your annual overhead will be $108,000. Your gross margin will have to be more than sufficient to cover that amount. It will have to cover that and still leave you a bit of profit.

You might expect your opening inventory to cost you about $40,000. If you plan to turn that amount over three times a year, your annual cost of goods will be $120,000. If your markup on that cost was 100%, or $120,000, it would only allow you $12,000 net profit. (Gross profit of $120,000 less operating overhead of $108,000 = $12,000.)

If that looks like a lot, let's consider net margin as a percentage of your annual turnover of $240,000:

$12,000 net profit ÷ $240,000 turnover x 100 = 5 % net margin

Five percent net profit isn't high enough to build up much of a rainy day fund, or create a cash reserve that will help you expand your business. If you aspire to make more profit, you'll have to look at a higher markup than the 100% used in this example.

## How Low Can You Go?

Pricing is a strategic part of owning a boutique. The right price is not always the lowest price at which you can afford to sell an item (or worse, lower), or you may price yourself out of business.

Trying to keep up with someone on the other side of town who advertises blow-out prices could be unwise, particularly if that business has made the error of pricing their goods too low and building in a profit margin so lean that they're on the verge of bankruptcy themselves.

You also have to factor in perceived value, which is a funny but proven thing. Sometimes you'll actually sell more of an item if you price it $5, $10 or even $50 higher, because the consumer will attribute greater value to it. Tread carefully though and be fair when you decide how much your customers will be prepared to pay for each item; never run the risk of letting them feel taken advantage of.

## 4.5  Hiring Your Staff

Finding, hiring and training a strong sales staff is one of your most important jobs. Even if you only need one other person during your first few months of business, that staff member is an essential component of your boutique, a significant factor in your success, and an ambassador for your product and service.

Initially it might just be you and one other part-time person working your shop. Very small stores in quiet communities can still get away with hanging a sign on the door that says "Back at 2:00," and locking up when they need to use the washroom or pop out for a sandwich.

As your business grows and more customers start visiting your shop, you might need one full-time person (in addition to yourself) and one part-time person. You might be gone for a week at a time on buying trips, and if you open weekends and a few evenings, you'll quickly find that the work week has more hours than a single person can handle.

Getting the right staff takes time, but that time is an investment worth making. A good decision will pay off for years to come; a bad decision may cause you a fair bit of grief and anxiety. Here are some tips for making it easier.

## 4.5.1   Finding Applicants

To find employees, you have a number of options. The most important and cost-effective thing you can do is tell everyone you know that you're looking for help. You might know someone who knows someone who knows someone who would be just right.

You can also place a classified ad in the local newspaper at a cost of anywhere from $50 to $200, or you could simply put a discreet, tasteful sign in your shop window and be patient.

If you place an ad, make it as specific as possible. If you're determined to employ only people who have experience with retail fashion, specify that requirement. You'll save yourself a lot of time going through resumes if you make what you want clear up front.

Normally you'll ask applicants to fax or email a resume with a cover letter. It might work to have them drop the information off in person as well. If you're busy with customers you won't be able to give the applicant much time, but if they arrive during a quiet period you'll be able to observe their appearance and manners and see how they react to your store and merchandise.

This needn't be as formal as the actual interview, but it can provide a good opportunity to get a general feeling about them and whether they'd be a good fit for your boutique. It's pretty simple from there. If you like the resume, you call them in for an interview.

## 4.5.2   The Interview

We've provided a list of questions below to use if you're not sure what to ask potential employees. Based on their answers to your questions and their overall attitude, you'll quickly get a feeling for them, positive or negative, and an idea as to whether you'd want to work with them.

- Why did you leave your last position?

- What did you like most about your last position? Least?

- What are your future ambitions?

- What do you love about fashion?

- Do you like working with the public?

- How would you define good customer service?

- What is your greatest strength?

- What is your greatest weakness?

- How do you get along with co-workers?

- How would you resolve a problem with a co-worker?

- How would you resolve a problem with an employer?

- How would you describe a good employee?

Try to imagine the applicant not just through the eyes of an employer, but through the eyes of a customer as well. Would you want this person serving you? Are they gracious, polite and helpful, or do they ooze an eye-rolling attitude that makes you want to scream?

Because labor laws vary from state to state and province to province, you'll want to check on the local regulations. It is also an offense to discriminate based on gender, ethnicity, religion and age. Nolo.com has detailed and useful free advice online about fair and legal hiring practices. Visit **www.nolo.com** (click on the "Business & Human Resources" tab, then on "Human Resources").

## Checking References

If the interview goes well, you should ask them for references. This is especially important if they haven't been recommended by someone you know personally. If they don't have references from previous employers because they've never had a job before, ask them if it's okay to contact their teachers or volunteer coordinators. Friends and relatives aren't ideal references for obvious reasons.

Some people ask for references but don't follow up on them. They think it's enough for someone just to have references. I don't agree. Almost anyone can come up with the names of three people who will say something nice about them. I always call references and try to ask very pointed, specific questions (see examples below).

- How long was the applicant in your employ?

- What were his/her duties?

- Did he usually perform them to your satisfaction?

- Did she ever surpass your expectations?

- Did you consider him to be honest, trustworthy and reliable?

- Did you ever get the chance to observe her handling a difficult customer?

- Did you have complaints from customers or other employees?

- Would you hire her again?

This last question is the most important one to ask an employer. If they hesitate, you'll know there was something about the person that makes them less than enthusiastic about the idea of working with them again. On the other hand, I've had people say, "I'd hire her again in a second" or, "I actually wept the day he resigned."

You can ask a teacher or volunteer coordinator the following alternate questions:

- How long did the applicant work with you?

- What were her strengths?

- What were some of his weaknesses?

- How did he resolve conflict?

- If you were running your own business, would you consider hiring her?

## What to Look For

Experience is a lovely thing, but in my opinion it isn't the most important deciding factor. There are boutique owners who would caution against hiring someone with limited retail sales experience. While it's true that those people don't necessarily have a related background, I think that the selling skills can be learned.

The most important quality you can look for in potential employees is a winning attitude. Some people just shine, regardless of age or experience. They look alert, as if there's someone at home in their brain. You just know that they'll use good judgment and make the right decisions if something new to them should crop up. That kind of spirit is rare, and if someone who shows it approaches me for a job, I'm going to take a chance on them, even if they've never had a similar job before.

Here's another thought: sometimes it can be easier to train people from a blank slate. They've never acquired bad habits, like approaching every customer with a flat "May I help you?" Instead, you'll be able to explain why it's better whenever possible to greet customers in a friendly, personable way and strike up a conversation.

## 4.6  Legal Matters

Few people who set out to own a boutique do so from a business perspective first. It would be rare for someone to think, "I'd like to start up my own business. Hmmm. What kind of business? How about a fashion boutique?"

The people who start up a boutique business do so because there's something about the product or service they feel drawn to. They choose to sell clothing because they love fashion, have a sense of style and want to immerse themselves in that world. The business side of it is something they usually learn along the way, because they have to in order to survive.

That was the case for boutique owner Beth. She loved yoga and the way it made her feel. She began to make and sell yoga products as a way to share her enthusiasm with other people. It was with a sense of surprise after a few years that she began to think of herself as a business person.

In this section we begin to walk you through the practical aspects and legal matters you'll need to consider when you start a boutique of your own. "Business is not a dirty word," confides Beth. "Use your own business as a way to extend your personal interpretation of ethics. You'll be happier and your customers will respond."

### 4.6.1  Business Legal Structures

Your boutique will need to be set up under one of the following legal structures: sole proprietorship, partnership, LLC or corporation. Below is a brief overview of each, with a discussion as to their advantages and disadvantages. You should also talk to your accountant and your attorney about the various pros and cons of each legal structure.

## Sole Proprietorship

In a sole proprietorship, you are the exclusive owner of the business. You alone are responsible for all decisions regarding the business. The profits are yours alone, but so are any debts!

A sole proprietorship is the simplest and cheapest way to set up a boutique business. You don't have to consult with anyone as to what color to paint the walls, whether to take on a relatively unknown new designer's line, or whether to give your star salesperson a raise. It's your baby.

Conversely, there is no one to turn to if you want help making a decision. Sure, you can solicit the opinions of family, friends and your spouse (and you'll find that most people are very forthcoming with these), but you're the one who has to live it. If you suspect a regular store visitor of shoplifting, you will have to decide whether to ask that person not to come back to your shop. You'll have to decide whether to return an order of turquoise sweaters that you remember ordering as teal.

## Partnership

Legally the partnership is very similar to the sole proprietorship, but the financial responsibilities, tasks and profits must be shared with your partner(s). It is not uncommon for two people to decide to become partners in a boutique business; however, groups of more than two in such a small business are relatively rare and more difficult to hold together.

A partnership is not unlike a marriage. When it works well, the partners' different skills and abilities complement each other to make a solid, effective unit. There is one more person to raise capital and assume financial risk; one more person available to share busy weekend and evening shifts.

"My business partner and I make an ideal match. Our personalities are opposites and they complement each other. We have clearly defined roles: I supply the creative energy, while she has that necessary attention to detail," says Sue.

On the other hand, when it doesn't work well it can be bitter, stressful and filled with petty and not-so-petty resentments. When things go bad the only escape is to dissolve the partnership, sell half of the business to one partner, or sell the entire business to a third party.

"My partner was my best friend and she helped give me the courage to start my own business, but it was still a challenge working together and trying to agree on all the decisions that had to be made. After five years she graciously asked me to buy her out. We sacrificed the partnership so that we could save our friendship," says Beverly.

> **TIP:** If you want to run the business on your own but require financing from another person, you can also choose to set up a limited partnership, in which you run the day-to-day business, and the partner simply invests money.

Remember that in a partnership you are responsible not only for your own actions, but those that your partner makes. This includes not only intentionally dishonest practices, but absent-minded errors as well. If your partner is making an order for blouses and incorrectly writes a 100 where a 10 should be, you're both responsible for paying for the additional product that you receive.

It helps to clearly delineate what responsibilities will fall under each partner's jurisdiction. Conflict can be avoided if your roles are clearly defined and you both know that one of you is responsible for the buying and merchandising, while the other attends to the books and budgets, for example. Have an honest heart-to-heart with your would-be partner. Discuss possible scenarios to make sure you have a similar business perspective. If you disagree about basic concepts, chances are that one of you would always be compromising in the business.

You should also see an attorney about drawing up a partnership agreement — the business equivalent of a pre-nuptial. This can be as detailed as you both want it to be, and can include the areas of responsibility that you wish to assume. It can also offer a contingency for dissolving the relationship should it become necessary.

## Corporation

Legally, the corporation is more complicated than the other business structures and for that reason it is not as common a choice for many boutique owners. The corporation is more costly to set up and to maintain. If you do think that a corporation is the best route for your boutique, you should definitely get the help of a lawyer to set it up.

You are not personally liable for the debts of the corporation. The corporation is a separate entity, a citizen of sorts, which means that business can continue even if one of the principals should die. This is one of the features that makes the corporation more attractive to investors and lending institutions; it is felt to be more viable over the long term.

Another distinctive aspect of the corporation is that principals own stock in the company and they can transfer ownership by selling their stock. Additional capital can also be raised by selling stocks.

## Limited Liability Company (LLC)

The limited liability company offers many of the advantages of the corporation but is less complicated in structure. Like a corporation, it exists as a business separately from the person who owns it, and it offers your personal finances protection. Unlike a corporation, it can't issue or trade stock. You can't sell stocks as a way to raise capital. Nor can it have shareholders or a board of directors.

Like a corporation, an LLC can protect your personal finances from any unfortunate business difficulties. If someone chooses to sue the business, they sue the business and not you personally. It is more costly to set up than the sole proprietorship, though, and does not offer the advantages associated with issuing and selling stocks.

## 4.6.2   Licenses and Permits

You will require a number of licenses and permits to start your boutique, which will vary depending on where you decide to open for business. You'll at least require a basic business license before you open to the public, and you may require building permits for any construction that you need to do.

If your region has sales tax, you will need to register to collect and remit it to the authorities, and you will also need to register with the IRS and Department of Labor if you plan to hire employees.

Once you have a location decided on, you should also check with the municipal jurisdiction as to any local laws regarding opening and closing times and traffic concerns. Some downtown areas, for example, don't allow large trucks in the city center within certain hours, which will affect the way your suppliers can deliver product to you.

The Small Business Administration website can assist you with researching the licenses and permits needed for your area. Visit **www.sba.gov/hotlist/license.html**.

Another good resource for permit and licensing information is Nolo's Business & Human Resources site. Go to **www.nolo.com**. Click on the "Business & Human Resources" tab, then on "Starting a Business," then on "Obtaining Licenses & Permits."

# 4.6.3   Insurance

Your business will need to be insured to protect you, your staff, customers and products against any number of unfortunate scenarios such as theft, fire or onsite accidents. You will want to talk to an insurance professional to find out which types of insurance you will need for your boutique, but below you'll find the most common ones.

## Business Premises and Contents Insurance

This will cover your actual boutique and contents. If you rent space, the landlord/owner would normally pay for insurance on the property.

## General Liability

Covers injury to clients and employees on your premises or elsewhere either in the performance of duties for the company or involving activities of the company.

## Life, Disability, Accident and Illness insurance

Provides you with a source of income if you should become seriously ill or disabled and unable to run your business, or provides for your family if you are their main source of income.

### Business interruption or loss-of-income insurance

This will allow you to continue to pay the bills if your business is closed down by damage due to fire, flood, or other catastrophe.

### Partnership Insurance

Protects you against suits arising from actions taken by other partners in your business.

### Workers' Compensation Insurance

Covers employees' medical and rehabilitation expenses, as well as their lost wages resulting from an on-the-job injury.

The Small Business Administration website explains the various kinds of insurance and why you might need them. (Visit **www.sba.gov**, then click on "Tools", and look for "Publications" under "Library & Resources." On the next web page, choose "Management and Planning Series" then scroll down to #17.) To discuss insurance in general and the specifics of different policies you should contact an insurance agent or broker.

## 4.6.4   Accounting and Taxes

Chances are you'll want to hire a professional accountant before you purchase an existing business, buy into a franchise, or submit loan applications to any potential lenders. In addition to helping you with the financial documents needed for your business plan, a good accountant can advise you on start-up and operating costs.

Your boutique probably won't need a full-time bookkeeper once it's up and running. You might learn to do basic books yourself, or have someone come in a few times a month to stay on top of it.

A popular accounting software program for small businesses and the self-employed is Quicken Premier Home and Business, which allows you to manage your payables and receivables, and run reports to see where you are at financially.

"I wasn't prepared for how much time it would take to do the paperwork, the responsible part, the uncreative part of the job. I underestimated the amount of administrative work it takes to run a business," confesses boutique owner Wendy. Consider yourself forewarned!

Your boutique will of course have to pay taxes on its profits, and depending on your local tax laws, you may have to collect sales tax from customers as well. We strongly recommend hiring an accountant or tax specialist to advise you on the taxes you will have to pay, and the proper documentation required.

The kinds of taxes you have to pay and when you have to pay them are going to vary according to your business and its location. The one certainty is that you will need to pay some kind of tax, so you'll have to develop the discipline and the systems for putting tax money aside on a regular basis so it's there when the bills are due.

Even with the help of a professional it's a good idea to have a basic understanding of taxes yourself. In the U.S.A., visit the Small Business Administration Site to familiarize yourself with the different kinds of tax regulations. You can find information on taxes at **www.sba.gov/ smallbusinessplanner/manage/paytaxes**. In Canada, you can visit the Canada Revenue Agency website at **www.cra-arc.gc.ca**.

# 4.7 Your Grand Opening

The most exciting day you'll experience is your boutique's grand opening. All of the hard work and research has paid off. The buying is done and you've received enough stock to open the store. The build-out is done, the walls are freshly painted, the permits and licenses are all in place, and you've got the necessary staff to help when things pick up speed.

To ensure your day is all you imagined it to be, start planning several months in advance. Think of it like planning a wedding, or any other "grand" event. You'll want to have a checklist of who you will contact and what you will do each week leading up to your opening.

It's wise to actually open for business a couple of weeks, even a month or two, before you have a "grand opening" celebration. This gives you

time to receive straggling stock, get used to the cash register and have all your systems flowing before you invite large numbers of the public and press to check out your shop.

Alternately, you can set aside time to train your staff in advance before you open. It's not that they don't know how to do their jobs, but they need to know how to do it your way. You'll include this money in your start-up funding.

There are many ways to make a grand opening a successful launch pad for your business. Most boutique owners make the grand opening a slightly festive affair, although you don't want to go overboard with party food and drink. Food and beverages and clothing tend not to mix too well!

You may choose to circulate flyers to let people know where you are and when you'll be open, or advertise on the local radio or in newspapers to draw customers into your boutique. If you can generate an article in a local newspaper to promote your grand opening, so much the better. Section 5.5 will teach you what you need to know about sending press releases and spreading the word.

**TIP:** Take photographs of yourself, staff and the boutique on opening day. These will be a component of the promotional material you'll send out to the press down the road.

You might choose to discount your product by 10% for the day or two of the opening, or arrange some kind of two-for-one purchase plan. Or you could have a brief in-store fashion show so guests get to view the garments on models.

The idea is to give potential customers a good reason to make the effort to come and visit your store for the first time. Hopefully they'll like what they see and decide to pop in on a regular basis. And even better, they'll tell all of their friends what a great new shop they found.

# 5. Running Your Boutique

As a consumer, your experience of a boutique is likely that it is a fun and easy-going place to work or be. You may not be aware of the frenetic activity, long hours, and emotional investment percolating just under the surface to maintain that sense of simplicity for the sake of the customers.

Even if you spend a year designing and developing your new boutique, plan on another year of operating glitches before you get all the bugs worked out. You will always be adapting to the changing needs of your business and your customer and always striving to be the best you can be.

# 5.1 Merchandizing

While deciding on the design and layout of your boutique is an excellent opportunity to spread those creative wings, it's important to remember that merchandising is not all about personal creativity, but also about function and representing the essence of your boutique. It will contribute to how customers perceive and remember your boutique, as well as help to define their shopping experience.

Design refers to the more permanent features that make up the overall look of your boutique, such as flooring, color, lights, and all those things that might be considered interior design, as discussed in section 4.1.4. Layout is more closely related to how merchandise is displayed and presented in departments and sections.

Your visual merchandising will have a major impact on your sales, so make your store inviting and interesting. You will be constantly coming up with new ways to present your stock to clients in a way that is fresh and attractive. Here are some tips from our experts on this vital aspect of running your boutique.

## 5.1.1 Arranging Your Product

Let the layout of your shop (along with the garments you sell) do as much of the selling for you as possible. This means you should organize the stock in such a way that it's easy to find. Most often this will involve simple logic. If you feature five or six designers, you'll probably want to keep each collection together, especially because a good designer will have planned her line so that the pieces merchandise well together.

Some boutiques that feature many different labels will keep trousers together, skirts somewhere else, suits in their own corner, and evening dresses together on a small rack. If your store is for both sexes, it makes sense to keep women's wear on one side and men's wear on the other.

Don't crowd your racks with too much stock — keep it uncluttered. Think about where the hangtag (the card tag that shows the price and size) is on the garment, and hang the style in such a way that it's easy for the customer to find her size and to see the price without having to ask for help.

# Ways to Group Your Product

Within each product category, keep all the stock of a given style in one general area, if not on the same rack. One of the most effective ways to group your styles (in my opinion it's the "cleanest" looking) is to group first by color, and then within that grouping, by size.

Let's say you buy a wool turtleneck in black, grey and red. The black should hang together, with size extra small at the front, then small, then medium, etc. The other two colors will also be grouped with sizes in sequence, either next to the black ones or elsewhere in the store.

Some shops choose to group by size first and color second, so all of those medium turtlenecks would be together (black, red, grey) and then the mediums would all be together (black, red, grey), etc. This quickly looks busy — it may be easy to find a customer's size, but the overall effect is not restful on the eye.

Another alternative would be grouping all pants together by size, all shirts together by size, all sweaters together by size, etc. That means that every style of pant you carry in size six, in every color, will be shown together on a rack, usually separated by plastic rings that indicate what the size is.

This type of merchandising is most common in discount or consignment shops where the buyer tends to acquire a vast assortment of product style, but not much volume in any given style. If your boutique is either of these two styles, this type of merchandizing could be very effective for you.

# Coordinate to Sell

Now let's say you've bought a Paul Smith trouser style in three colors: ivory, chocolate and black. To keep it simple, you could merchandise these on a single long rack, with all of the ivory together, then the chocolate and then the black.

However, a more effective strategy would be to hang the ivory trousers in a section with ivory shirts and sweaters that coordinate with the pants. Then you'd put the chocolate and the black trousers nearby but on their own rack or stand, likewise grouped with shirts and sweaters or jackets that work well with them.

When you position coordinating pieces so that customers will find them near the things they go best with, the entire outfit naturally sells itself. A customer who came in looking for a red turtleneck might buy the red turtleneck, the grey turtleneck and the red and grey plaid skirt they both look great with.

> **TIP:** Effective merchandising also includes putting small point-of-purchase in a visible location near the cash desk. When your customer is standing at the counter ready to buy a suit that costs several hundred dollars, he'll be more likely to notice the tie pin or cuff links or socks that work with it.

For an excellent, helpful article about the visual merchandising of your store and how it can add to your overall brand's impression, you can read an article on "Developing a Powerful Store Image Through Effective Visual Merchandising online from Retailer News. Visit **www.displays-store-fixtures.com/visual-merchandising.htm**.

## 5.1.2 Window Displays

Window displays have become a highly specialized art form. There was a time when window-dressing consisted of little more than a mannequin or two in well-coordinated outfits. These days the best windows are more sophisticated and the presentation revolves around an overall theme or concept that goes beyond the clothing itself.

One of the most interesting windows I've seen recently doesn't feature any clothes at all; merely white paper sculptures of dresses hanging on a line that from a distance look like summer frocks. It's very eye-catching and works to draw people into the shop, which is what you want. (It also means that the staff won't be asked to undress the mannequins so a customer can try on the window outfit!)

You might choose a single mannequin standing next to a table and a vase of flowers, or you might choose to display a few outfits suspended from invisible wire, or laid out on a chair or a flat surface. You might choose to make your windows seasonal in theme, with Christmas trees or fat pumpkins or large red hearts, depending on the time of year.

TIP:  The window design should reflect the personality of your overall brand. A highly sophisticated boutique would probably not feature Santa and reindeer in a December window.

When you arrange your window displays, make sure that the mannequins you feature in your windows aren't noticeably old or chipped. As the first impression your boutique makes on the passerby, these mannequins should be the best you can afford. Save your secondhand mannequins for displays elsewhere in the store, but don't let your windows embarrass you.

You should always make sure that the window display is illuminated at night. Margaret employs this technique in her boutique, since she knows that many of the area's tourists walk by her shop on their way to restaurants after business hours. Customers frequently tell her that they noticed her window as they walked past the night before.

We suggest you start paying close attention to the most effective window displays in your town and in the other cities you visit. Take photographs for inspiration and make notes for later reference.

If you don't feel that creating effective windows is one of your strengths, see if one of your employees has a natural talent for it, or take some training yourself. Many cities have schools that offer programs in fashion arts, including design and merchandising. Often these are quite extensive and the curriculum that falls under the name of "fashion merchandising" actually covers a lot more about the business of buying, selling and managing retail fashion.

If you're hoping to take a night school class that will help you merchandise your boutique, look for classes specifically in visual merchandising or visual display. Otherwise, having a professional visual merchandiser come in to do them every two weeks would be a worthwhile investment.

If you want to consult professionals, there are firms that can help manage your window installations or teach you the basics of how to make effective displays. Example includes Dynamic Resources Inc. at **www.dynamicnyc.com/services_installations_windows.html** and Strategic Merchandising Partners Inc. at **www.smp-inc.com**.

# 5.1.3   Signage

No matter where your boutique is located, be it shopping mall, strip mall, city center or retail village, the one marketing tool you won't be able to live without is signage, both storefront and interior.

A storefront sign is your boutique's packaging, telling potential customers what you're all about and presenting them with a first image. There are several style options with storefront signs. In some cases, the type of sign that you use will be subject to the rules and regulations of mall management, or city by-laws, so be sure to check with mall management or local officials before commissioning the creation of any signage.

Sign prices vary from a couple of hundred dollars to into the thousands. Many sign makers also have a monthly rental plan. Here are a few of the common exterior sign choices.

## Illuminated

These are the plastic signs common in malls and strip malls, which have the store's name painted or decaled on, and fit into a casing with fluorescent bulbs used to illuminate the sign.

## Awning

An awning with the boutique's name on display functions well as storefront signage, and adds a touch of elegance to your street-front boutique.

## LED (Light Emitting Diode) Signs

This newer kind of retail signage is digital, which allows you to use it as a static nameplate, or to scroll and flash multi-colored messages. These are generally wired to your computer and are very easy to use. Be aware that these could boost your electricity bill, though!

The purpose of interior signage is less about selling the business, and more about moving product. There are several options with in-store signs that don't have to break the budget. As much of this signage will change with promotions and prices as needed, one solution is to purchase or rent sign stands. These metal stands hold cardboard signage — the large ones are self-standing, while the smaller ones are meant to sit on clothes racks and desks. These signs can be professionally designed with your boutique's logo, or hand-printed by you and your staff.

There are also several illuminated signage options for indoor use, such as panel signs, which are essentially smaller versions of illuminated storefront signs. Also, don't overlook the timeless sandwich board. It's mobile, and the message is easily changed.

For more information on the types of signs available or to find a sign maker, look "Signs" up in your Yellow Pages, or review the options at an online sign store such as Letterbank (**www.letterbank.com**).

## 5.2   Effective Sales Techniques

Volumes have been written about how to be a successful salesperson, and in fact we'll recommend a few of them in this section. However, in my opinion the best sales strategy is simply excellent customer service.

Bend over backwards giving your customer better service than the competition — better service than they could ever have imagined — and the sale will follow. Selling is about making it easy for them to make the decision to buy. It really is as simple as that.

### 5.2.1   Greeting Customers

Make eye contact and smile as each new customer walks through your door. If you're already busy helping someone, taking a phone call or counting stock, a quick smile will let them know you've seen them and you'll be right with them. They'll feel welcome in your store as they begin to browse through your merchandise.

Say hello or whatever else pops into your head to make them feel welcome and that you're at their disposal. The object of the greeting is to make them feel welcome in your store and to let them know that you are there to provide assistance should they want it, but if they don't want your help they should feel free to browse.

The next line you speak should come naturally, and you should read the person's body language to try to determine how they feel about being approached. What you say is up to you. Some retail environments have begun to shy away from the classic offer of help — a straight "May I help you?" can sound stiff to some people. Other options are:

- Is there anything I can give you a hand with?

- Is there anything particular you're looking for today?

- Is there something I can help you with today?

- A more casual comment about the weather, the customer's fabulous shoes, etc.

Actually what you say is less important than how you say it. If it feels natural to you, it will probably come across as the right kind of greeting. It's important when you train your staff to encourage them to use an approach that feels natural to them, not a memorized line that every salesperson uses to greet every customer that enters your store.

If their response to your initial greeting is warm and friendly, go ahead and start up a conversation. If they look wary, or as if they're on the verge of fleeing from the store, give them a few minutes to explore on their own and get a sense of your merchandise.

If they tell you that they're just looking, or simply say that there is nothing you can help them with, smile and say something like, "Okay, my name is Chris if there's anything I can help you with." Then go back to polishing chrome or unpacking stock or doing anything else that requires your attention. You don't want to stalk them through the store if they want to be left alone to look. If you're always about two feet behind them, they might decide they're uncomfortable and move on before they've even looked at everything you have to offer.

## 5.2.2   Making the Sale

When a customer expresses interest in trying a garment or outfit on, make sure they have everything they need to complete the look. For example, if they are wearing tennis shoes to try on a business suit, and you carry shoes, get them an appropriate style in their size so they can see a total look. You never know — you might end up selling the shoes, belt, or bag you offer with the outfit.

When a man I know went into a boutique to find a suit for an upcoming wedding, the sales staff promptly helped him find a suit that he liked enough to try on. He didn't need to buy a new shirt, tie or shoes, but they offered to bring him each of those items to try with the suit, just so that he could envision the total look of the suit as he might wear it to the wedding instead of over his T-shirt and running shoes.

Guess what? He was so taken with the pieces they chose as a complement to the suit that half an hour later he bought not only the suit, but the shirt, the tie, and the Italian leather shoes they'd brought him to try. Far from feeling that he'd been pressured into the sale, he was appreciative of the excellent considerate service, and has been back to the boutique many times since.

## The "No Pressure" Approach

We've all been into shops, usually at the higher end of the market, where the pressure to buy is so thick it's like paint running down the walls. It can be a very unpleasant environment to shop in. We strongly advise you to discourage this kind of attitude in your staff and in yourself. Instead, be as friendly, knowledgeable and helpful as you can.

In Margaret's boutique, she and her staff are knowledgeable about their product and about the designers who create them, but no one who works in the store is ever aggressive in their sales attitude. They'll show the line and talk about each piece to prospective customers without ever pushing anyone to try anything on.

Does her technique work? Margaret says yes. In her very first month of business a tourist walked in and spent $3,000. A year later, the same customer returned and spent another $4,000!

A good salesperson sells only to those who want to buy, and occasionally, through friendly, helpful advice will turn an indecisive shopper into a buyer. Don't try to sell to someone who doesn't want to buy.

If they like what they see, it's likely they'll come back another day when they are in the market for what you are selling. That is, they'll come back if you haven't hounded or pressured them.

## Honesty and Integrity

Oddly enough, the concepts of honesty and integrity aren't automatically associated with successful selling. However, they should be. Most people can spot a phony when they see or hear one. Please, be upfront with your customers. If the horizontal stripe is less than flattering, or the shade of taupe washes him out, don't brim with fake enthusiasm.

Now, that doesn't mean that you should give your opinion when it isn't solicited. If they seem happy enough with what appears to be a less than ideal choice, smile and thank them for their business as you ring in the sale. It's possible the stripes are motivation to make the next diet work, or that the taupe will be a gift for someone who wears neutrals better.

But if they ask what you think, call on every diplomatic resource in your repertoire. Don't necessarily make a face or say, "I don't think so." Suggest other things for them to try. Bring a solid top, or one with a different pattern, or a color with more life to it.

What if they ask you to help them choose between two outfits? One clearly makes them look better, but the other one is significantly more expensive and therefore a better sale for your boutique. Be honest anyway. Tell them which one you actually like best. Customers are smart enough to connect the dots. They'll realize that it would have been to your advantage to steer them to the higher-priced outfit. Your honesty and integrity will shine and there's a better chance that they'll become a loyal customer down the road.

## Point-of-Purchase Add-ons

When a customer is ready to purchase, make sure you remind them about the things you carry that they might have forgotten. If you're selling a dress shirt to a man, make sure he knows about your tie selection. If you sell lingerie, you might offer small bottles of special detergent for washing delicate items. Little things like this can increase each individual sale, and will significantly improve your sales volume over time.

> TIP: Make sure you carry a variety of these products that are easy sale add-ons. If you don't remember to buy them, you won't have them in stock when you need them.

# Know Your Terminology

If a customer flies through your door on her lunch break and says she needs a pair of olive green Capri trousers or a black dress with princess seams, you should know exactly what she's talking about and point her in the right direction immediately.

Here are some basic terms you'll want to be familiar with.

*A-line:* Also known as trapeze-shaped, this refers to a dress or top slightly shaped like a triangle – the base is notably wider than the shoulders. It is an effective style for women who want to disguise broad hips.

*Bomber:* A short jacket, usually with a waistband and cuffs, inspired by the type that fighter pilots once wore.

*Car coat:* Longer than a jacket but shorter than a full length coat, the hem of a car coat usually stops between the thigh and the knee. It was intended (you guessed it) to be worn in a car so the extra fabric would not bunch up or drag on the floor.

*Capri pants:* Women's trousers designed to end near the mid-calf, or just below the calf

*Classic:* Clothing and footwear that does not date or go out of style (neither is it ever especially in style). The cut, cloth and colors are so basic that they endure over the decades. Generally for the more conservative shopper.

*Empire Waist:* This look is named for the women's dress style of France just after the revolution, with a waistline much higher than the natural waist and in some cases directly below the bust line. Think of Napoleon's Josephine in all her sheer white dresses.

| *Form-fitted:* | Basically what it sounds like. Designed to flatter a trim figure with a lot of tailoring details like darts and seams. |
|---|---|
| *Hipsters:* | Low-rise trousers or skirts that sit very low on the waist, right around the hip bones. |
| *Princess* | Vertical seams that run up the front of a dress, |
| *Seams:* | coat or blouse on either side of the imaginary center front line. These are usually curved at the bust line. They give a fitted effect and a longer look to a garment. |
| *Silhouette:* | The most dominant aspect of design that changes from season to season (and radically from decade to decade) is the silhouette or "cut" of a garment. |

Still not sure you have all the lingo down? For additional fashion and garment terminology check out the About.com Fashion Glossary at **http://fashion.about.com/od/glossary** or the Fabric Link Textile Dictionary at **www.fabriclink.com/Dictionaries/Textile.cfm**.

## 5.2.3   The Little Extras

You should take advantage of every opportunity to excel at customer service. The little things you do will leave customers with a positive impression that will make them think of you next time they go shopping. It will likely bring them back to your boutique and remind them to tell their friends about the great new shop they discovered.

For example, if you don't know for a fact that the item is for the purchaser, offer to gift wrap it for them. Tell them how to care for the product. Ask if they'd like to join your customer file, to be advised of special sales and promotions. Above all, make sure you thank them warmly and say that you hope they'll come back again.

Even if the customer doesn't purchase anything, make sure that as they leave you thank them for visiting your store. Invite them to come again.

You might mention that you're expecting a new shipment the following week, or that you're planning a big sale next Monday.

Do everything you can, in a friendly casual way, to make sure that every customer will come back again. Sooner or later there's a strong chance that they'll buy from you. And who knows? The customer who buys nothing during their first, second or even third visit might end up being your best client some day.

Boutique owner Margaret has a clear vision of what excellent customer service means to her. If a regular customer can't make it into the store within regular business hours, Margaret will arrange to open late to accommodate them. Without the presence of other customers she's able to give them highly personalized one-on-one service.

Another way to offer value to your clients is to stay abreast of trends, as well as becoming knowledgeable about the items you carry. Read fashion magazines so you can suggest a number of ways to work an outfit with accessories etc. Learn about the designers you carry and what might have influenced them in their creation of a collection.

TIP: Make it easy for your staff to acquire the same kind of knowledge by holding regular staff meetings, and buying magazines for the staff room.

The manufacturer is required, in most countries by law, to include a label with instructions for cleaning and pressing the garment. This may be in the form of words or color-coded symbols, telling consumers if a garment is machine washable or requires dry cleaning. You should get in the habit of familiarizing yourself with the care instructions of the styles you carry, so that you can tell a customer when they ask, or even as you're wrapping up their purchase.

Learning about wardrobe consultation can be a major addition to your skill set too. By studying the elements of a functional wardrobe and by learning how to attractively dress certain figure types or color palettes, you'll be able to offer your customers better service. A personal consultation will give your customers another reason to come back to your shop.

Moreover, if you help your customer look more fabulous than she's ever looked before, her friends are going to start asking her where she shops. A good-looking, well-dressed client is likely to lead to referrals, which will inevitably increase your sales.

For more advice on sales, there are many excellent books available including the _FabJob Guide to Become a Super Salesperson_, by Harry Frisch, and _No Thanks, I'm Just Looking: Professional Retail Sales Techniques for Turning Shoppers into Buyers_, by Harry J. Friedman.

# 5.3   Store Operations

From handling your money to suspecting theft to taking inventory, day-to-day life in the boutique goes better if you have spent some time thinking about your policies and procedures. Here are some tips to get you going.

## 5.3.1   Handling Cash

Although fewer people are using cash today, it's vital that you know the basics of handling it. Even the most basic registers will calculate change these days, but you should also learn a simple method for calculating change yourself.

You should use this method for counting out change as you give it back to the customer; even if your cash register has done the math, this method is more courteous and more professional than just dumping a handful of coins into their hands. It allows the customer to count with you and be assured that the change is correct.

Here's how it's done. Let's say a customer's purchase with tax totals $26.42. She gives you $40. Instead of using a calculator to subtract the purchase from the cash given to you, just count forward from $26.42 to $40, using the largest denominations available.

In this case you will take 3 pennies, one nickel, two quarters, three dollar bills and one ten. You'll give it to the customer like this, saying: "Your total was $26.42." Put the pennies into her hand, saying "$26.45." Add the nickel. "$26.50." Then the quarters, "$27.00." Add the three dollars, "$30.00," "and ten makes $40. Thank you." Counting to yourself this way will become easy with time.

## Your Cash Float

You'll need to open each morning with a "float" in the drawer, which is a predetermined amount of cash that lets you make change for customers' cash purchases. The size of your float will depend on the size of your business, but $100 - $200 in a good mix (change, ones, fives and tens) should get you started.

Count your float each morning to double-check that the correct amount is in there, to make your life easier when cashing out at the end of the day. If you use some of your float for petty cash purchases (say you need to buy toilet paper for the staff washroom), record how much cash you take from the till with a note. When you come back with the purchase, return the change and staple the receipt to your note so that you include it in the count at the end of the day.

You'll count out a new float at the end of the day and put it in a safe at night, leaving the cash drawer open so anyone passing by will see that it is empty. Then count the remainder of your cash and make sure it tallies with the day's cash receipts as per your journal. This should get deposited into your bank account as soon as you can. Don't leave cash sitting around.

## Your Cash Register System

You can spend as little as $100 on a new electronic cash register that will tally a customer's purchases, calculate the taxes appropriate to your region, make change, print a customer receipt, and generate a daily sales journal for your accounting records. These basic systems are ideal for small businesses, but many limit the number of departments or categories you can enter, and may not allow you to enter as many PLUs (price look-ups or individual price points) as you require.

For about $250 you can get a system that includes a barcode scanner. Barcodes are printed right onto price tags or labels, and they contain the product or style number, usually the specific color and size, as well as the retail price. The code can be read automatically by the register or system scanner.

Barcodes offer the advantages of speed and greater accuracy, because there's less room for error. If you purchase stock from larger vendors, many will provide a bar coded tag on the merchandise when it arrives. While this might sound like a dream come true, remember that each PLU or "price look up" item will initially need to be entered into your computer so that your cash system will reference the correct item and price. With new items coming in every few weeks, this can add up to quite a bit of data entry work.

Starting at about $350 you can purchase a more advanced register with a greater number of PLUs. These higher-end systems also often come with PC Link Software that will connect to your computer for generating a variety of reports. These systems can perform sophisticated tasks like:

- Provide you with reports for pinpointing your best customers, best sales staff and most lucrative product lines

- Track your inventory, allowing you to monitor stock levels and issue P.O.s

- Report on sales by employee for calculating commissions and bonuses

A complete point-of-sale (POS) system connects the scanner and cash drawer with inventory and accounting systems. POS systems can be quite advanced and quite expensive. Expect to spend from $2,000 to $3,000 on a POS.

You'll probably find that more of your customers these days want to pay by credit card or debit card than by traditional cash or check. Make sure you make it easy for customers to buy by choosing a cash system that will let you take as many forms of payment as possible.

## Gift Certificates

Gift certificates are an excellent promotional tool, and a great way to get free word-of-mouth advertising for your boutique. Although most gift certificates are sold during the Christmas season, it's important to always have them available for your customers.

You can have gift certificates made at most local print shops, where they will help you design a stylized certificate complete with your boutique's logo.

You can decide to carry certificates with specific denominations, such as $20 and $50 certificates only, or have blank certificates in which you handwrite the amount. A handwritten certificate provides customers with more flexibility on how much can be purchased, but it also opens the door to forgeries.

## Bogus Bills

With color printer technology, counterfeiting is more common and convenient than it once was. Get in the habit of looking at the cash you are given. Your bank can give you tips for checking money to make sure it's real, or you can purchase a machine or pen that will authenticate bills. These are available from many of the same suppliers who provide cash registers.

## 5.3.2   Security Issues

Most people are honest and are not out to steal from you, but it only takes one or two to cause your business harm. This brief section will advise you to take precautions and protect your boutique from theft. "The only really devastating thing that happened in twelve years was that my store was burglarized on Christmas Day. The police arrived within four minutes, but by that time the thieves had already made off with 80% of my stock," Wendy told us.

Make sure you get an alarm system installed and that you use it. Depending on your location you might choose some kind of window bars as well. If you're in a mall, you should pay attention to briefings from the security people. Learn what you can from them; they exist to help you and can provide you with a number of crime-prevention tips.

In addition to doing what you can to protect your business from break-ins while the store is closed, you're going to have to prevent shoplifting too. Train your staff to watch people carrying large bags. Keep small items, the size that can slip into a pocket, near the cash desk where you and staff can keep an eye on them. You can also install a mirror so that you can watch the door from the back of the store.

If you run a busy boutique, monitor the number of items that someone takes into a fitting room and make sure that they come out again with the same number. Some boutiques limit the number to about three pieces at a time; others give customers a numbered tag to take in with them that indicates how many garments they have.

> **TIP:** Watch for hangers that no longer have a garment attached to them; these can be a sign that the tank top or trousers got stashed in a shopping bag.

If you carry expensive or designer merchandise, you can't afford to lose even one piece of inventory. Consider installing security cameras and getting a system where a clothing tag beeps if someone tries to remove it from the store.

Also, not all theft is external. While most of your employees will be great, you should always be cautious and keep the staff you choose to be key-holders (i.e. those with keys to the store and know the alarm code) to a minimum. You can use the links provided here to find information about shoplifting laws, tips on how to prevent retail theft, and resources for purchasing security equipment for your boutique.

- *How to Prevent Shoplifting*
  **http://retailindustry.about.com/cs/lp_retailstore/a/ uc_delaney1_3.htm**

- *Shoplifting Statutes by State*
  **www.pcgsolutions.com/shoplifting_statutes.htm**

- *Apparel Search Retail Security Directory*
  **www.apparelsearch.com/retail_store_security.htm**

## 5.3.3   Taking Inventory

Your annual financial reports will require you to take an inventory once a year. Inventory refers to the dollar amount of stock you have on hand at any given time. "Taking inventory" refers to the process of physically counting this stock and calculating its worth.

It's actually an excellent plan to take inventory more than once a year. Some businesses even do it quarterly. Remember, the inventory reflects the worth of your business — this is something you want to be informed of. Also, doing a regular count will draw attention to stock that isn't moving, styles you're extremely short of, or other sales trends.

It's common to do your inventory at the end of the season when you don't have much stock to count. Ideally you'd plan for it after a clearance sale and before any new stock arrived, to make for a bit less work.

## Running an Inventory Report

If your computer software allows you to enter purchase orders and receive goods into the same system that rings in your sales, it should have the ability to print detailed inventory reports any time you wish. These will be by style or at least price point, and I advise purchasing a system that will allow you to enter by color and size as well.

However, these reports will be accurate only if all of your entries from receiving to purchase transactions are absolutely accurate, and if you experience no shrinkage due to shoplifting or internal theft. If your cash register is not sophisticated enough to provide inventory reports, you need to calculate it manually (we'll show you how below).

It's also common — but vexing — for a physical count of inventory to differ slightly from the computer's idea of what is in stock. Therefore use your computer's inventory reports, but do not rely on them absolutely. You must back them up with a physical count. This will allow you to check on the report's accuracy, and investigate reasons for any discrepancies such as staff errors, etc.

## Doing a Physical Inventory

The inventory will need to be counted while the store is closed, so that no transactions are made during the count. No sales, no receiving, no returns. The doors should be locked so no curious customer can pop in for a look. The key to taking an accurate inventory is to simplify the actual count as much as possible by dividing your store into very small sections. This way your counters won't have to count very many items at one time, and the margin of error will be reduced.

Use a count sheet like the one shown on the next page and make multiple copies of it. Securely tape the count sheets to every rack, shelf, stand, bin, window, display unit, drawer, stockroom rack, etc. Make sure you include any places for keeping customer holds. You need to account for every single piece of merchandise in every conceivable location.

# Inventory Count Sheet

| Count location: | | Date Taken: | |
|---|---|---|---|
| Sheet #: | | Checked by: | |
| Counted by: | | | |

| Style # | Description | Retail Price | Quantity | Extension |
|---|---|---|---|---|
| | | | | |
| | | | | |
| | | | | |
| | | | | |
| | | | | |
| | | | | |
| | | | | |
| | | | | |
| | | | | |
| | | | Total: | |

# Inventory Count Sheet – Filled

| Count location: | West rack one | Date Taken: | December 31, 2008 |
|---|---|---|---|
| Sheet #: | 001 | Checked by: | R.S. |
| Counted by: | D.M. | | |

| Style # | Description | Retail Price | Quantity | Extension |
|---|---|---|---|---|
| SW002 | Tweed jacket grey | $100.00 | 4 | $400.00 |
| SW002 | Tweed jacket lime green | $80.00 | 5 | $400.00 |
| SK110 | Sweater crochet black | $50.00 | 6 | $300.00 |
| SP050 | Wool pant grey | $50.00 | 6 | $300.00 |
| SP050 | Wool pant black | $50.00 | 2 | $100.00 |
| | | | Total: | $1500.00 |

**TIP:** The "extension" on the count sheet is the retail price multiplied by the number of that item in stock.

On each sheet you must enter the actual quantity of items counted on that rack, shelf or stand, beside the price. Note the quantity as soon as that location has been counted so you're less likely to remember it incorrectly. If you have the same style at two different price points (e.g. the lime-green color is not selling and you have marked that color only down 20%), then list them on separate lines.

Each sheet should be numbered so you can account for them all later. The person who did the count should initial the sheet, and a second person should double-check that count, also initialing the sheet. The extension and the total for each sheet can be tallied at a later date, even when the store is open for business again, since it is just doing the math.

When your count sheet is filled out, it should look like the sample. The dollar total per sheet can be written on a master document that lists the count sheet numbers in sequence, with room to put the location, and a column to enter the dollar value. At the bottom, add up the value of all the sheets and calculate a grand total.

Make sure you find and note all of the individual count sheets on your master list! The grand total should be checked against your computer's inventory report, if you are using one.

## 5.3.4 Setting Hours and Policies

You will want to have your policies in place before you open so your customers and your employees will know where you stand. Store policies should reflect your personal philosophies, and should also reflect the needs of your customers and employees. For example, if you think closing on Sunday works best for your business and employees, do so — although you'll be subject to mall hours if your boutique is in a mall.

Many storefront boutiques keep hours that catch both the lunch and after-work crowd, which is usually around 10 a.m. to 8 p.m. Many boutiques will stay open later on Thursdays and Fridays, to correspond with employee paydays and when shoppers stay out later or shop for weekend events.

Developing written complaint policies is also important. They provide you and your employees with guidelines to follow for common issues, such as merchandise returns. Also, keep in mind that complaints may arrive via the phone, letter and email. Determine who will handle these, and in what manner. A form letter can work well for many letter and email complaints.

No amount of diligence or countless hours in your boutique will protect you from customer complaints. The fact is that you can't please everyone all the time. But this doesn't mean that you can't attempt to resolve issues to the customer's satisfaction every time. Here are a few tips on effectively handling complaints.

### Take responsibility

Even if the customer isn't "always right" all the time, the fact is that a customer complaint is usually something that was overlooked as a potential problem. Let the customer know that you sympathize, restate the issue, and thank them for helping to improve your boutique.

### Don't create a problem

When approaching a customer with a complaint, don't lead with, "What's the problem?" Maybe there isn't a problem; just a misunderstanding. By referring to the situation as an "issue" you can keep the complaint from escalating to the "problem" level.

### Treat complaints as a learning experience

Complaints can be tiring, but when treated as an opportunity to learn new ways to improve your boutique, they can be a real boost to your day.

### Resolve immediately

Don't let the resolution to a customer complaint drag on too long. Evaluate the situation, consult your policies, and present an immediate solution. Customers will appreciate that you value their time.

## 5.4   Managing Your Staff

The boutique business is a "people" business in more ways than one. You not only have to please your customers, you also have to lead your team of employees. So how do you motivate your staff to be the best they can be? Here are some ideas on effective scheduling, communicating with staffers, and keeping them happy and productive.

## 5.4.1   Scheduling

Scheduling your employees should be done with attention to your busy times, what needs to get done (shipments arriving, lunch rushes, etc.) and what you can afford. It would be ideal to have a huge staff on at all times in case you get swamped, but the reality is that you will have to pick and choose what times most need the extra coverage.

Your busiest times are normally evenings and weekends, but afternoons during the week could generate a fair bit of traffic. How busy you are is often seasonal, as well — the months of November and December will probably see crowds of people milling about in your shop, and depending on your location you might notice a surge during the summer tourist season.

It's handy to have two people to open up in the morning, which can include yourself. Together they can get the cash register prepared, vacuum and tidy the store, as well as assisting the customers who appear early.

Around 11 a.m. it's nice to have a third person in to cover lunches, so you don't have to stand at the counter eating. If you're busy, it could be essential. The thing to remember is that in a busy shop you'll want at least two people available on the floor at all times, and more during the peak customer periods. Make sure that a key-holder is always scheduled in for the start and end of each day.

To help you see how boutique scheduling works, the facing page has a sample staff schedule for a medium-sized boutique open weekends and two evenings a week. Note that there is a minimum of two people on during open hours; an extra to cover lunches, and more on Saturday for peak traffic times.

Labor laws dictate the required break periods, lunch or dinner breaks, and shift maximums or minimums that may affect your scheduling. You can familiarize yourself with your legal obligations as an employer and locate your State Labor Office at **www.dol.gov/esa/programs/whd/state/state.htm**. In Canada, you'll find this information at **http://bsa.canadabusiness.ca** (click on "English" then look for "Hiring Employees or Contractors").

## Sample Staff Schedule

| | Mon. | Tue. | Wed. | Thur. | Fri. | Sat. | Sun. |
|---|---|---|---|---|---|---|---|
| **Sara** | 9:45 a.m. – 6:15 p.m. | 9:45 a.m. – 6:15 p.m. | Off | Off | 9:45 a.m. – 6:15 p.m. | 9:45 a.m. – 6:15 p.m. | 11:30 a.m. – 5:30 p.m. |
| **Jon** | 10:00 a.m. – 6:00 p.m. | 10:00 a.m. – 6:00 p.m. | 9:45 a.m. – 6:15 p.m. | 9:45 a.m. – 6:15 p.m. | 10:00 a.m. – 6:00 p.m. | Off | Off |
| **Mai** | 11:00 a.m. – 3:00 p.m. | Off | 11:00 a.m. – 3:00 p.m. | 10:00 a.m. – 2:00 p.m. | 1:00 p.m. – 9:00 p.m. | 10:00 a.m. – 2:00 p.m. | Off |
| **Greg** | Off | 11:00 a.m. – 3:00 p.m. | 10:00 a.m. – 6:00 p.m. | 1:15 p.m. – 9:15 p.m. | 1:15 p.m. – 9:15 p.m. | 12:00 p.m. – 6:00 p.m. | Off |
| **Rose** | Off | Off | Off | 1:00 p.m. – 9:00 p.m. | 11:00 a.m. – 3:00 p.m. | 11:00 a.m. – 5:00 p.m. | 12:00 p.m. – 5:00 p.m. |
| **Terri** | Off | Off | Off | 5:00 p.m. – 9:00 p.m. | 5:00 p.m. – 9:00 p.m. | 11:00 a.m. – 3:00 p.m. | 1:00 p.m. – 5:00 p.m. |

## 5.4.2 Good Communication

Most successful boutique owners and managers have regular staff meetings with their employees. Depending on the size of your business, these might be once a week or once a month. Obviously these should be set outside of business hours, either early one morning before the store opens or one evening after it closes.

You should use the time to update your staff as to new product that's expected and how best to sell it, any promotions you plan to run, procedural issues, etc. Share your excitement over the fabulous new designer you discovered at the Paris show, or tell them about the new part-timer who'll be joining the team for the Christmas rush.

---

### Commission and Bonus Structures

To commission or not to commission? This is a tricky question. Obviously, some kind of financial incentive works to motivate your staff, improving their salesmanship and your daily sales turnover.

However, commissioned salespeople can be aggressive in their manner to customers and competitive with their fellow staff members. The resulting environment isn't always pleasant to shop in or to work in. It isn't always the case, but things can get that way.

A bonus system is a softer way to provide that incentive. Maybe you give $100 a month to anyone with personal sales over a certain level. Obviously, you'll need a fair and accurate way for tracking whose sales are whose, whether you go this route or the commission route.

Another idea that won't result in a competitive spirit is to pool a more substantial bonus, maybe $250 to $500 depending on the size of your staff. If sales go over the monthly target, they each get a share based on the hours they worked that month. You can also offer a staff discount on merchandise of 10-30%, so that your staff will be encouraged to promote the boutique's merchandise in their look as well.

---

Any meeting works best if the communication is two-way. Make sure you ask them for their feedback; don't just give a monologue at every meeting. It's a good idea to circulate an agenda a few days before and let people add to it if there are things they want to discuss. That way they'll all feel more involved, and having an agenda as your guide tends to keep the meeting shorter and more focused.

Boutique owners Beth and Jacqueline found that regular staff meetings and requesting staff input has not only increased sales but improved morale. Their cash register has a field for entering how the customer found out about the store, and by reminding staff to use that field (instead of skipping it), they were able to gauge the effectiveness of an ad they'd run in the local paper. By explaining why the information was important, they were able to get the staff excited and involved.

## 5.4.3   Evaluating Staff Performance

You should evaluate your staff periodically and let them know how they're doing. This might be after a new employee has been with you for three months, or it could be after six months. The review should be at least an annual event with each employee. You can use a form similar to the sample provided in this section.

This is an opportunity to discuss raises, bonuses and room for improvement. It's also a great time to ask each employee if they're happy with their job, if there's anything they suggest doing differently, and what their ambitions might be. You might find that someone has a secret longing to dress your windows, or to step into the role of store manager.

If you think it will open up better communication, ask the employee to fill out the evaluation form in advance about their own performance. Then go through it item by item with the employee during the review, and compare areas where you differ in evaluation.

The results can be surprising; sometimes an employee will be harder on herself than you might be. She might think that she's mildly inefficient or lacking in professionalism, whereas you think she's strong in both areas. Of course the opposite can be the case, too — a chronically late employee might think she's extremely reliable.

---

## Sample Performance Evaluation Form

| | | Not at all | | | | Exceptional |
|---|---|---|---|---|---|---|
| 1. | Does the employee demonstrate that they are punctual and reliable? | 1 | 2 | 3 | 4 | 5 |
| 2. | Is the employee's work reasonably free of errors? | 1 | 2 | 3 | 4 | 5 |
| 3. | Is the employee quick to catch on after being shown something? | 1 | 2 | 3 | 4 | 5 |
| 4. | Is the employee willing to take on new tasks as requested? | 1 | 2 | 3 | 4 | 5 |
| 5. | Is the employee generally courteous, pleasant and alert? | 1 | 2 | 3 | 4 | 5 |
| 6. | Does the employee get along well with other staff, management and customers? | 1 | 2 | 3 | 4 | 5 |
| 7. | Does the employee demonstrate good selling skills? | 1 | 2 | 3 | 4 | 5 |
| 8. | Does the employee demonstrate good product knowledge? | 1 | 2 | 3 | 4 | 5 |
| 9. | Does the employee demonstrate a good understanding of company procedures? | 1 | 2 | 3 | 4 | 5 |
| 10. | Does the employee show initiative in bringing new ideas to the organization? | 1 | 2 | 3 | 4 | 5 |

---

# 5.5  Attracting Customers

Once your boutique is gearing up to open, it's time to tell the world — and most importantly your target customers — how to find you. There are a number of ways to do this, from the cost-effective word of mouth, to flyers and postcards.

You should definitely get business cards and letterhead stationery printed with your business name and contact info, logo and tagline, if you have one. You might also choose to have your own hangtags printed with the store logo, address and website.

Business cards are often the first image someone gets of your business. In addition to cards for yourself, and possibly your manager, you may also want to have some "blank" ones that your staff can write their name on and personalize.

Make it count by designing a beautiful, interesting card on good cardstock with simple, easily read fonts. Don't make it too busy, but be sure to include the basics, like your boutique's name, address, phone number, and website. Make sure it complements your website, your sign or store colors, and any advertising you do. For stationery, choose the best quality paper you can afford, or one that is designed to best represent your brand.

When you are first launching your boutique, you can entice people to come check it out by printing a discount offer (10 or 15% off) on the back of the card. Many businesses do this, and it may work with a boutique selling not-too-expensive merchandise.

Think hard about whether price is a concern to your target market, though — when you are selling designer goods, sometimes price is not a motivating factor. Consider whether an offer of a free gift to take home might be more effective in your niche. You should also have a time-limit on using these coupons, since you don't want giving away "free stuff" to cut into your profit once you have an established clientele.

### 5.5.1   Paid Advertising

Advertising is the space you buy to promote your boutique in a newspaper, magazine, popular website, or radio and television spots. There's also direct mail advertising, where you mail your ad directly to the consumer.

If your budget allows an extensive ad campaign, you should find a talented ad agency, communications or design firm and let their creative brains go to work for you. Advertising does not come cheap and you don't want to waste print space with an ad that looks amateurish.

Many businesses start their advertising with a display ad in the Yellow Pages. While this may not be the best route for a high-end fashion boutique, if your boutique sells something very specific, such as maternity clothes, used children's clothing, or vintage, it may be a worthwhile use of your advertising dollar.

Most boutique owners we spoke with agreed that their advertising budget was best invested with a print ad in the entertainment weeklies, glossy city magazines or the kind of city-guide magazines that are published for visitors. The lifestyle or fashion section of your city newspaper can also be worthwhile, or a community paper in a small town.

Since your goal is to get the attention of the busy readers, make the ad as large as your budget can reasonably afford, and use color when possible. Choose an ad position that will stand out on a page that will be seen by as many members of your target niche as possible.

For example, in late August or September your entertainment weekly might have a back-to-school fashion spread — these pages can be a great place for a hip boutique ad. Or if the magazine's editorial calendar suggests that they'll feature an article about swimsuits in mid-March, then that might be a perfect opportunity to promote your bikini boutique.

Choose a bold, tasteful image for your print ad, ideally a photograph of one of your pieces or a very stylish fashion illustration. The ad's design should reflect your brand's identity. Mention your boutique name and location, as well as the phone number and operating hours. List your website address if you have one.

If your ad has a specific purpose in mind, make sure you boldly say "Grand Opening!" or "Huge Sale!" and give the date and time. You might invite customers to bring in the ad for an additional 10% savings. This is smart for two reasons: those who see the ad have additional incentive for visiting your store, and you'll be able to directly track the success of your ad by the number of people who use it to purchase.

Costs to run an ad in a newspaper or magazine are going to vary widely, but you can plan on at least a few hundred dollars per insertion. The higher circulation of the print medium you choose, the more expensive that space will be, so your freebie community newspaper will probably cost less than the entertainment weekly. Other factors that contribute to cost will be the size and location of your ad.

Some newspapers will help you lay out an ad if you don't have one ready-made, usually for an additional 15 to 20 percent of the purchase price. Otherwise, a freelance graphic designer is who to contact. You don't want to blow your budget here, but if you're going to advertise, make the best, most professional impression that you can.

There are other, more expensive options for advertising like radio or TV spots, but these tend to be quite pricey, and our experts suggest you'll probably get more results for your investment with a well-chosen print ad.

If you want to break away from magazines or newspapers, other more feasible options include seasonal postcards that are direct-mailed to your customers once you have customer base, or buying screen time at your local theater (these ads run like a slide show before the movie starts). You can have a graphic designer put together your postcard, or talk to your local printer about having one designed in-house. You can also try online companies like Modern Postcard (**www.modernpostcard. com**), which offers postcard design and mailing services.

Also, don't forget that your boutique sign is the first thing clients will see that attracts them, and is a form of advertising in itself. It should be of a size appropriate to your shop exterior, and it should be prominently displayed, whether mounted on the front wall or hung above the door, and the logo should be well designed. You want the name to be legible, and the style of the lettering, sign construction itself, colors etc. should all reflect the other design elements of your shop.

If you are set back from the street (say, in a strip mall) you can draw more attention to yourself with a sandwich board or rented announcement board. Just be sure to check with your local bylaw department to find out if these are regulated in any way.

## 5.5.2   Free Publicity

Advertising may be expensive, but getting an article written about you costs little more than photocopying and postage. Your local fashion journalists write and print stories in newspapers and magazines, and are featured on TV and radio programs — why shouldn't they write about you?

Not only is this exposure free, but it tends to have more impact on the savvy consumer than paid advertising. The voice of the press is invaluable, so make sure your boutique gets attention from the media. You do this by sending out press releases (single sheets of info) or press kits (info, news and photos) to let them know how unique you are, how special your product is and how amazing your service is.

There's a lot of competition for precious editorial space, so you'd better make sure your press kit really shines. You'll get the ball rolling with a press release, and include some good photographs to generate interest. Then every time you get press exposure, you clip that page from the magazine or newspaper and make photocopies of it. These become part of your press kit, and your next press release is accompanied by examples of the things that journalists have already had to say about your shop.

Your press release headline should read like an actual newspaper headline, and catch the editor's attention by addressing the important, newsworthy facts immediately. So what's newsworthy? That's up to you and your imagination, but you can read the publication regularly to get an idea of what gets printed.

One boutique owner that I worked with years ago had some creative ideas about getting attention from the press. When a shipment of fitted Moschino denim skirts arrived, she had three of us dress up in the tight skirts, paired with Moschino logo T-shirts. The local newspaper had office space just down the block, so we walked into the building, hand-delivered the press kit to the fashion editor, and walked back to the shop. We got her attention, and our boutique got a small feature a few days later.

The body of the press release is usually written in the third person, again, as if it were already an article. The next page has a sample of a press release. Yours will go on your business letterhead and should be personalized for each fashion editor you approach.

## 5.5.3   Word of Mouth

This kind of "advertising" also costs next to nothing. If you give your customers a great shopping experience with an interesting, well-priced

# Sample Press Release

FOR IMMEDIATE RELEASE
Contact: Tracey Taylor
*Phone:* (111) 555-1234
Email: tracey@stylehaus-boutique.com

## NEW BOUTIQUE OFFERS AMAZINGLY AFFORDABLE DESIGNER-WEAR

*Stylehaus: Designer Fashion at Unbelievable Prices*

The truly well-off and super-style-conscious purchase the highest quality designer fashions each season, wear them a couple of times… and then what?

They bring them to *Stylehaus*, of course!

Stylehaus is a new consignment shop, re-selling premium quality fashion to members of the public who couldn't otherwise dream of affording genuine Armani, Prada or Miu Miu. Located in the fashionable uptown district of Anytown at 111 Wheeler Ave., it is both accessible and affordable.

Stylehaus accepts only high-fashion clothing in excellent condition with the original designer label still intact. Most of the merchandise has barely been worn and appears brand new.

What would have originally sold for several hundred dollars can now be had for $20 or $30. An outfit that looks like it costs thousands can be put together for under $100. Stylehaus carries women's wear, men's wear, children's wear, jeans, evening gowns, coats, suits, shoes and accessories. If it is truly designer fashion in pristine condition, you'll find it here.

### ###

Your fashion-conscious readers will want to know about this unique resource for affordable designer style. For more information about Stylehaus, or to schedule an interview with Tracey Taylor, please phone us at (111) 555-1234 or visit **www.stylehaus-boutique.com**.

product in a pleasant environment with excellent service, they will want to tell their friends.

Still, it isn't as important to them as it is to you, so it's not a bad idea to reward them somehow for bringing new customers to your door. During your first month of business you could hand out a business card to customers who make a reasonable purchase. The card could have the customer's name written on the back and an expiry date.

If one of your customer's friends brings the card in, they get a ten percent discount on their first purchase. You record the sale and who referred that customer, and then call the original customer to let him know that you're giving him a store credit of an additional ten percent of that sale.

Don't overdo the discount idea, but don't be fooled into thinking that you're giving too much away, either. Remember that as the end of a season approaches, much of your stock will get discounted in order to sell. Better to use a strategic discounting system on select purchases that will generate customer traffic, thereby minimizing the likelihood of your having a lot of stock left at the end of the season.

## 5.5.4   Customer Files

You might have heard that 20% of your customer base will be responsible for 80% of your business. It's absolutely true and it seems to be true whatever business you're in. You want to make sure that you're identifying those customers who are your "80/20" and looking after them well.

Many successful boutiques build a list of their customers. When you make a purchase there, they'll ask if you'd like to be notified about sales and other special events. If you say yes, they enter your contact information into their file. At one time this information was kept on index cards; now most often it is computerized.

A boutique owner or manager can use this information to stay in touch with their key customers. For example, on a quiet Tuesday morning you and your staff can go through the files and call or email regular clients to let them know that all the spring merchandise is being marked down 20%.

You can also send out a mailer that entitles the recipient, as a preferred customer, to a discount off regular priced merchandise on a specified weekend. You might also choose to call customers and let them know that you've just received an extensive shipment of fall sweaters, boots and winter coats.

The most sophisticated customer files also record every purchase for future reference, so you can call with information such as, "We've just received a blouse that would look great with the trousers you bought last month." The customer file can even act as a wish list. Let your customers know that they can give you their wish lists, then send their family members in to your store to do gift-buying, and you have a record of exactly what they want in the desired sizes and colors.

## 5.5.5   Your Website

The Internet is a powerful retail tool, and the value of an effective website should not be underestimated. Not all of the boutique owners featured in this book have a website, but many do. Some have a site enabled for e-commerce, where clients can actually place orders and pay on the site itself.

Those who have a well-designed e-commerce site say that the sales it generates contribute significantly to their overall business, in some cases outperforming any one brick-and-mortar store in the group. A good website will cost you initially, but it could pay for itself very quickly.

## What to Include

Your boutique's website should include:

- Your logo

- Your location (a small map helps)

- Your phone number

- Your hours of operation

- An email address to contact

- Your mission statement

- A brief description of the products you sell

- Accepted methods of payment

- Store policies

- A way to collect email addresses and phone numbers to add to your client database

You may also choose to add some of the following features:

- A way to buy merchandise or gift certificates online

- Monthly specials or coupons

- A virtual tour video

- Information about the merchandise you stock

- Photos of the interior and exterior

- Testimonials from happy and/or celebrity clients

- Profiles of you and your best employees

- Fashion and wardrobe advice

- A careers/jobs page

Remember to make your website consistent with the image of your boutique. Don't underestimate the power of words, colors and images to take your potential client "virtually" into your environment.

Your website is as important a first impression as your storefront is. Make sure it's attractively designed, easy to navigate, well written, and most of all, that it suits your brand identity.

## Getting it Made

A website can cost you a couple of hundred dollars or several thousand dollars. An e-commerce site that accepts orders and payment online will run you more than a basic site will.

So many people are fluent in web design these days that your friend or neighbor or relative might offer to do you a site for next to nothing. Be sure to tread carefully; but if their offer is genuine and you've seen their work, go for it. You can also find a wealth of web designers local to you by looking in the Yellow Pages under "Computers & Electronics", or "Internet Website Design."

If you want to post your project out for competitive bids from all over the world, consider a site like Elance Online (**www.elance.com**). This will expose your request to creative freelance web designers from all over the world. Note, however, that you won't be putting money into your own community, which will in turn support your boutique down the road.

## Marketing Your Site

One of the first things you'll want to do, even before you build your website, is register your domain name, which is what people will type into the computer to go to your website: www.YourBoutique.com. For a small monthly fee you can host your site through a service company, register a domain name, and get your site listed on search engines so that clients can find you. One company that provides this service is GoDaddy (**www.godaddy.com**).

Be certain all of your printed marketing material contains your web address, and include it on all your press releases. You can also update your website to include clips of media coverage you get.

## 5.5.6   Trunk and Fashion Shows

Hosting private or public events in your boutique is a great way to get people through the door. Even non-fashion events such as book readings or wine tastings can work in this way, provided the event is the type to draw in your target market.

### Host a Trunk Show or Sample Sale

In most cases, a boutique will only purchase select items from a designer that they believe will sell the best. But when you love the designer, wouldn't it be great to carry the entire collection? Well, that's what happens at a trunk show, if only for a few days, or one exclusive evening.

At a trunk show, the designer brings in all his or her merchandise to the boutique for a limited time, either in a variety of sizes, or in sample form. The name "trunk show" comes from the past, when designers would carry around their latest samples in a large trunk. The trunk show is often a semi-social event, to which the retailer invites select clients to sip champagne, nibble hors d'oeuvres, and of course, buy the latest fashions.

The trunk show is promoted as a short-term event when customers can come in, meet the designer or his or her sales representative, and get advice on choosing a garment. If you have an established client base, you can contact them personally and invite them to your trunk show.

The trunk show also offers the customer a chance to see the entire design collection in one place. How you arrange sales with the designer is up to you — you can let them sell direct and just benefit from the publicity, or you can ask for a commission of their sales.

Trunk shows benefit the boutique because they are good publicity, and because you don't have to buy the designer's entire collection to see what customers like. They also help you build a relationship with designers. You can list upcoming trunk show dates and locations on your website.

Sample sales are also a win-win-win situation for designers, boutique owners, and consumers. For the designer, it's a chance to unload the one-of-a-kind samples used to promote this year's line, or items they manufactured too much of for one reason or another. For the consumer, it's a chance to buy normally expensive designs at 25-75% off the usual selling price. For this reason, sample sales are usually a very popular event. Many sample sales are cash-only, and all sales are final. For the boutique owner it's great publicity and a chance to establish yourself as THE place to buy from.

When you promote your sample sales, don't forget to let buyers know what sizes you have available. While stock overruns come in every shape and size, true samples are made to fit model sizes 6, 8 and 10, not the average consumer.

## Have a Fashion Show

What better way to show off your new seasonal stock than with a private or public fashion show? It's usually not too expensive if you work with local models, and you stand to do a lot of on-the-spot business, as well as stand out from the boutique crowd.

You can open up your fashion show to the public, or agree that it will be by invitation only to preferred clients and media. This is a great way to make your regular clients feel appreciated, as they will be the first to select from the latest arrivals.

Serve food and drink, and have fun with the day/evening. Clients know they aren't in Paris or Milan, so you can make your fashion show as casual as you wish. Put together outfits for your models to wear in the same way you will coordinate them in the store. They'll look great, and clients who don't buy on the spot can come in and find those items accessorized together at a later date.

## 5.5.7   Having a Sale

Having a sale at your boutique is a great way to get people in the door, and an effective way to move merchandise. There is really no right or wrong time to have a sale, but seasonal and holiday sales are always sure winners. Just think of the opportunities to sell fall and summer clothes, or the party outfits you'll sell for Christmas and New Year's.

Common celebrations and events also represent a type of "sales season," such as graduation, wedding and back-to-school seasons. Also, off-season sales are a great way to move last season's merchandise. In fact, many consumers shop off-season, hoping to get a great deal in April on a winter coat that they won't need for eight or nine months. Beyond seasonal and holiday sales, anytime you find yourself with an overstock of a certain item is a perfect opportunity to have a sale.

The duration of a sale is up to you. Some retailers like to hold a sale only for a short period of time, such as a one-day sale, with the reasoning being that people will drop everything not to miss the sale. Others prefer to have a sale over an extended period, such as a week or even a month, to maximize customer interest and opportunity.

Here's some expert advice to help you get the most out of a sale:

- When having a sale on several items, place one sales rack at the entrance to grab shoppers' attention, and spread the rest of the sales racks throughout the store. This will bring the shopper into the store and past all of your merchandise.

- Don't bury sales stock in with non-sales items on a rack; customers should not have to work at finding sale items.

- In-house sales signs should not only shout that there's a sale, they should also be descriptive, with numbers that tell customers precisely what they will save, such as 10% off or 1/2 price.

- Using identical signage on sales racks allows customers to easily identify other sale items.

- Customers can't come to your sale if they don't know about it. Small ads in local newspapers, sales flyers and storefront signs promoting the sale will bring customers in and get them spending. Be sure that your ads state what's for sale, and at what savings.

- Be creative. Sales don't always have to be a straight savings of dollars. A sale can also be a buy-one-get-one-free promotion, or an opportunity to move some accessories that haven't budged, such as giving away a free pair of earrings with every purchase over $100.

# 5.6 Specializing in Bridal Wear

Are you a sucker for romance and beautiful gowns? If so, a bridal boutique could be a rewarding and profitable boutique specialization. As a bridal boutique owner, you'll help make the happiest days of a woman's life even happier. You'll also have a chance to be a part of the multi-billion dollar (and growing) wedding industry.

Weddings are a serious business. According to a recent study by the Fairchild Bridal Group, total spending on weddings has risen to $125 billion per year. Fairchild projects that wedding spending will continue to rise as the children of the Baby Boom generation reach marrying age.

The average formal wedding now costs $27,710. More importantly for bridal boutique owners, the Fairchild Bridal Group report announced that the average wedding racks up more than $2,000 spent on wedding apparel, including gown, veil, bridesmaid dresses, groom's tuxedo, men's formal wear, and mother of the bride apparel. Nearly $900 of that is spent on the wedding gown itself.

Although the bridal business can be profitable, it can also be challenging. Wedding gowns and accessories are emotional purchases. Your boutique will have to battle with department stores, discount bridal chains, and other boutiques. And you will seldom have a customer that is a repeat buyer, let alone a customer for life! However, if you do things right, you can find great success in the world of bridal retail.

## 5.6.1 Your Market and Location

As with any other retail business, the right location is vitally important to the success of a bridal boutique. And of course, what you want is a region of potential customers with a large population of up-and-coming brides, and not too much competition for that market.

To start, you can check with your local courthouse (or agency that issues licenses) to see how many marriage licenses have been issued in your county or region over the past ten years, and whether that number is growing or shrinking. This will give you an indication of the strength of your potential market.

According to recent research and census data, the average bride today is 25 to 27 years old. Check the age demographics of your area, as well as the number of weddings per capita. You can also compare those numbers to a national average to see where your region fits in. The U.S. Census Bureau has demographic and economic data at **http:// factfinder.census.gov**.

According to *Vows* magazine, a typical bride is willing to drive two hours from her home to visit a bridal store. That means your target market is anywhere within a 100-mile radius of your boutique location. That also means that all existing bridal stores within a 100-mile radius should be considered competition.

That doesn't mean that if your town or region has three other bridal shops, that you don't have a market. What you need to do is look for ways that the existing bridal shops are not meeting the needs of the buyer. Maybe the selection of gowns is limited, too high-end, or too low-end. Maybe their sales staff is pushy, or worse, apathetic. Maybe the prices are outrageous — even dressing rooms that are too small to turn around in can irritate an already stressed-out bride-to-be.

Once you have decided that there is a market for your bridal boutique, it is essential to pick a location that will attract customers. You can follow the general guidelines set out in section 4.1 on choosing a location, but also think about how that advice relates specifically to bridal wear. In addition, look for locations near other merchants that brides might visit early in the wedding-planning process, such as popular ceremony sites, reception locations, or jewelry shops.

Most brides — following the advice of wedding guides and magazines — start shopping for their bridal gown 6 to 9 months before the wedding. It's one of the first items on their wedding planning checklist. While locating near a florist might seem like a perfect idea, chances are that by the time a bride is choosing her flowers, she's long since ordered her wedding dress.

## 5.6.2   Your Gown Inventory

Once you've found the perfect location, you'll need an inventory of wedding gowns. Many brides have dreamed about their wedding dress since they were little girls. They expect they will know when they find "the one", and they won't settle for less than fairy-tale perfect. These are not easy to satisfy clients, so your inventory must be carefully chosen to (hopefully) satisfy each and every client.

### Types of Gowns

Bridal gowns generally fall into one of two categories: custom-order, and off-the-rack. Full-service bridal shops usually specialize in custom-order gowns. Bridal boutiques stock samples of gowns in different sizes and styles. Brides try on the samples and then order customized versions of the gowns, tailored to their measurements and specifications.

Custom-order gowns range in price from less than $600 to more than $5,000. You (the retailer) are billed for the samples when you purchase them, and must also pay up-front for each custom order.

This means that you must be prepared with sufficient working capital to cover your up-front costs, since you will be waiting for your money to come in. In order to off-set these costs, most bridal shops require a non-refundable 50% deposit from the client when the dress is ordered, with the balance to be paid on delivery. To further recoup costs, most boutiques sell their used sample gowns at discounted prices when they are no longer needed in the store.

Manufacturers usually require at least 60 days from order to receipt of the finished gown, which is longer than some brides can wait. For this reason, many bridal boutiques also carry a selection of off-the-rack gowns. Off-the-rack gowns are also popular with older or second-time brides who don't want a dress that's too formal. These gowns are less expensive, and will likely need alterations to attain a perfect fit.

Bridal wear is generally priced about 100% above wholesale (also known as keystoning). This means that a gown you pay $500 for will cost the client $1,000. This mark-up may seem high, but it is calculated to account for start-up costs and the length of time before a bridal boutique's investment in samples pays off.

## Choosing Suppliers

Carefully consider which gowns you want to carry. There are hundreds of great designers, but you will have to be selective. There are varied price points as well from designer to budget, so match your gowns to what you envision your customers to want.

You can access a list of many of the popular bridal gown manufacturers at TheKnot.com's wedding gown designer list at **www.theknot.com**. (Look for the "Gowns" link at the top of the page.)

When you have browsed bridal magazines and websites and decided what designers most appeal to you, you can contact the manufacturers directly to inquire about carrying their lines. Most of the designers' websites have contact information for retailers, and will put you in touch with a sales rep.

The major bridal trade show where the latest and greatest styles are put on display and you can place orders for the upcoming season is the National Bridal Market, held twice a year (spring and fall) in Chicago. Like most fashion trade shows it is open to retail buyers only (not the general public). Even if you don't plan to buy, you can get a sense of what will be in style in the upcoming months. Visit the website at **www.merchandisemart.com/nationalbridalmarket** to find out upcoming dates for this major event.

## What to Order

How much inventory you carry will depend on what start-up cash you have available, and what size of boutique you plan to open. It's important to note that many of the top wedding gown manufacturers require you to buy a minimum number of samples per season (twice a year). Minimums can range from 4 to 20 samples per season.

This may not seem like much, but it can add up. For example, if you are ordering 20 dresses at a cost of $500 each from only four designers, this could mean a required output of $80,000 a year just on samples. Stocking only eight designers will cost you $160,000 a year. In order to get around this buying minimum and still carry a decent variety of designers, local bridal boutiques have been known to partner up into buying networks and pooling their buying to meet the minimums.

Another option would be to become an authorized dealer of only a few lines, where you carry the full range of gowns from a handful of select dealers. In this case you will want to strongly believe in the designers, as their creativity and vision will make or break the success of your boutique.

For every bridal line you carry, you'll want to order a range of sizes to accommodate your clientele. The most popular bridal sizes are 10 and 12 (these will generally fit a woman who usually wears a size 8 or 10). You can also carry 8s and 14s if you have the money and the space.

Given the choice of ranging bigger or smaller, we'd suggest you will also want to stock some larger-size samples. It's fairly easy for a bride to pin a slightly-too-big dress to get a sense of how it will look. It's much harder to hold up a too-small dress and imagine if it will be flattering.

## Keeping Up With Trends

There are thousands of new bridal gown styles created each year, and it will be your job as a bridal boutique owner to stay up-to-date on the trends. A good way to do this is by reading the major bridal magazines, available at most newsstands. Among the most popular are:

- *Brides*
  **www.brides.com**

- *Modern Bride*
  **www.brides.com/modernbride**

- *InStyle Weddings*
  **www.instyleweddings.com**

- *Martha Stewart Weddings*
  (Click on "Weddings")
  **www.marthastewart.com**

Keep in mind that preferences differ by region. The minimalist look may be hot in one area, while elaborate princess styles are bestsellers in another region. Networking with other wedding professionals in your area, reading wedding coverage in local publications, and talking to actual brides will also help your gauge the local climate.

## 5.6.3   Other Products and Services

Typically, bridal boutiques offer a range of products and services for the bride and wedding party. Here are the most common ones.

### Bridal Accessories

Bridal accessories are a profitable sideline for bridal boutiques. When a bride tries on her gown, she will also want to try on shoes, a veil and/ or headpiece, jewelry and maybe even lingerie. The purpose is to try on not just a dress, but a whole wedding-day look.

Which shoes work best with this skirt length? Will a veil or a tiara work best with this dress? Does she need a slip or bustier? Use your expertise to help the bride pick out the perfect accessories to complement her dress, and your reward will be an up-sell opportunity.

### Bridal Party Wear

Dresses for bridesmaids and flower girls are generally custom-order gowns. The bride usually picks a dress for her attendants based on the color scheme and theme of her wedding (e.g. daytime vs. evening, modern vs. traditional). Once a dress is selected, the bridesmaids and flower girls are measured, and custom-made dresses are ordered from the manufacturer.

TIP: Many designers offer the same dress style with different sleeve, neckline, and skirt options. This allows for each atten-dant to choose a flattering style for her figure, while maintaining a consistent look for the entire bridal party.

Many modern brides opt for off-the-rack, cocktail-style bridesmaid dresses that attendants can wear again for other occasions. To meet this demand, bridal boutiques often stock an inventory of off-the-rack cocktail dresses in popular styles and colors. These can double as prom dresses/formalwear so you can expand your target market.

Some bridal boutiques sell men's formalwear or offer tuxedo rentals. In fact, the vast majority of grooms rent their wedding formalwear. However, keep in mind that offering tuxedo rentals will require additional overhead for inventory and additional staff to serve your male clientele. Analyze the market and competition in your area to determine if it makes sense to offer this service in your boutique.

## Wedding Accessories

Bridal boutiques can generate significant revenue by selling favors, place cards and other low-cost wedding paraphernalia. Generally, these items can be purchased wholesale for a low cost and sold at a healthy margin.

Examples of these miscellaneous items include place cards, guest books, disposable cameras for the tables, flower-girl baskets, ring-bearer pillows, and gifts for members of the wedding party.

## Alterations

Alterations are frequently needed to achieve the perfect fit. Wedding gowns are not in step with traditional sizing, and to complicate matters, all wedding designers have different sizing charts.

Some bridal boutiques hire full-time and/or freelance seamstresses to handle alterations for a small fee. Others refer customers to a third-party seamstress. Clients appreciate being able to do "one-stop" shopping at this hectic time in their lives.

# Online Shopping

Online shopping continues to increase in popularity. There are pros and cons to setting up your bridal store on the Internet.

## Advantages

- You don't have to pay rent or maintain inventory

- You are not limited by geographical area — anyone with an Internet connection can order from your boutique

- Because of lower overhead, you can sell merchandise at reduced prices and still make a profit

## Disadvantages

- Most brides want to try on their gown before they purchase, and sometimes a picture on a website just doesn't cut it

- Some brides aren't comfortable making major purchases over the Internet

- You can't provide the same level of service and personal advice as you can in a physical transaction

# Plus-Size Bridal

Half of all American women are size 14 or larger. With this in mind, more and more designers are recognizing the untapped potential of the plus-size bridal market. Research what local competitors are offering to plus-size brides. If you don't want to jump into the market blind, experiment by adding more plus-size styles to your sample selection to gauge the demand for plus-size bridal in your area.

# 5.6.4   Marketing a Bridal Boutique

When the buying is done and you've received enough stock to open the store, it's time to focus on getting those brides and their entourages into your store with a well-thought-out marketing plan.

# Online Marketing

According to Entrepreneur magazine, more than three-quarters of brides start their wedding planning online. With some savvy online marketing, you can make sure that potential customers find your bridal boutique when they're surfing the web.

To begin, your bridal boutique will benefit from a website, as explained in section 5.5.4. You might feature some photos of the gowns and products you carry, or at least the logos of your major suppliers. Testimonials from satisfied brides will also go a long way in swaying your potential clients.

You will also want to establish a presence on wedding-related websites so that your boutique's name will come up in a bride's initial search. The two most popular wedding websites are WeddingChannel.com (2.4 million unique visitors each month) and TheKnot.com (2.1 million unique visitors each month).

These sites offer a range of advertising options. For bridal boutiques, the most cost-effective advertising choice is in the local service directory sections. The cost of advertising in these directories starts at $30 per month. See the Advertising section of these websites for more information about options and rates. The pages are **http://wedding.weddingchannel. com/about_us/article_1317.asp** for Wedding Channel.com and **www. theknot.com/wp_cityadsales.html** for TheKnot.com.

# Other Marketing Ideas

Advertising in national bridal magazines can be prohibitively expensive for a small bridal boutique. A better bang-for-the-buck can be found with local editions of the wedding magazines mentioned earlier. Wedding Channel and The Knot also publish local-edition magazines.

Another advertising option is your community's local newspaper. Purchase an ad in the section that runs local wedding announcements. Many brides-to-be read these announcements regularly, looking for ideas for their own upcoming nuptials. You can also contact the Lifestyle section editor of a daily to obtain a calendar of what wedding-related features are planned.

Bridal fairs or expos are yearly events sponsored by major bridal-related companies, including department stores, magazines, honeymoon hotel chains and others. You can either rent a booth at one of these events, or sponsor a prize such as a free gown (sponsorship usually includes a booth).

These shows are two to three days in duration, and can attract up to 10,000 visitors a day. One of the largest bridal expos is The Great Bridal Expo, which sponsors events in cities around the country. The link below will take you to their latest tour schedule. The other two links are to help you find other local bridal shows.

- *The Great Bridal Expo*
  **www.greatbridalexpo.com/TourSchedule.aspx**

- *Bridal Show Producers International*
  **www.bspishows.com**

- *Wedding Shows*
  **www.weddingdetails.com/shows**

Finally, special in-store promotional events can help attract customers. Sample sales, seasonal sales and mark-downs are common promotions. Other ideas include raffles or contests with an attractive prize. To be eligible for the prize, entrants should have to make an appointment for a bridal consultation or make a purchase in your boutique.

## 5.6.5   Selling to Brides

Once you get those blushing brides into your store, the real work begins. According to the editors at *Modern Bride* magazine, most brides will visit four or five stores and try on 16 or 17 gowns before they find "the one."

To be successful in the bridal boutique business, you have to be able to close the deal. That means delivering great service and mastering the art of the bridal sale. Start by creating an environment that's conducive to pleasant shopping. Provide roomy try-on areas and seating for the bride's shopping companions. Offering water to the bride and tea or coffee to the waiting guests is also a nice touch.

Your boutique should smell pleasant (but not overwhelming) and convey a relaxed atmosphere to help the bride be herself. Organize your stock in a way that's easy to browse without the help of a consultant.

Most bridal boutiques prefer to book brides by appointment. This ensures that each customer will have your full attention and get the service she needs. Of course, if you've chosen your location well, you will probably also get customers walking in off the street to browse.

There's no way of knowing for sure who's a serious customer and who's just looking. It's frustrating to waste your time. However, good service can convert a browser into a buyer. And making the wrong assumption is a good way to lose a potential customer.

## Bride-Specific Sales Techniques

Of course, expert consultation is the service that sets a full-service bridal boutique apart from discount bridal stores and department stores. Bridal boutique staff should be true experts on the wedding industry. A trained bridal consultant should be able to show a bride options that she never would have found on her own.

Here are some ways to offer exceptional service in your bridal boutique:

- *Listen:* Most brides have specific ideas of what they're looking for.

- *Know your products:* Shopping for a bridal gown can be overwhelming. Your expertise can take a lot of the stress out of the process for your clients.

- *Give tactful advice:* If a customer asks your opinion about an unflattering gown, be diplomatic. If you think a different silhouette or style would look better on her, position it as a positive. Instead of telling her the sheath dress makes her hips look wide, tell her the A-line will showcase her lovely hourglass figure.

- *Be patient:* The average bride tries on many gowns in multiple stores before deciding.

- *Practice the art of the up-sell:* Put together a whole wedding-day look, complete with shoes and veil and jewelry. Accessories can make a beautiful gown look even better. If you do your job well, you may end up selling a complete wedding ensemble instead of just a dress.

- *Be size-savvy:* Wedding gowns run small, so brides should always order at least one size up from their normal dress size. Check the designer's sizing chart prior to ordering, and never let a bride or bridesmaid order a too-small size because she is planning to lose weight. It will only lead to heartache and hassles.

- *Be on your best behavior:* The Internet has created a whole new type of word of mouth. Wedding websites like WeddingChannel. com and TheKnot.com have very busy message boards where brides post complaints about bad wedding vendors and sing the praises of good ones. Treat every customer as if she will be posting an account of her experience for brides all over the world to read.

- *Be a girlfriend if needed:* Some brides are miles away from their mothers and bridesmaids, and are shopping for gowns on their own. Offer to help do up zippers, buttons and bustiers, and do your best to make them enjoy the solo experience.

# Handling Common Objections

It's unlikely that the bride is going to love the first dress you bring out to her. Be patient and listen to what she truly wants.

Here are some common objections you'll hear from clients on a daily basis, and how to interpret them to your advantage.

### "It's too expensive."

Work with the bride to better understand her budget. Suggest lower-cost alternatives if available. If the bride is simply trying to maneuver you down on price, reassure her that your prices are as good as (if not better) than your competitors.

You may want to tactfully ask what the approximate budget for the wedding is. This way, you can point out to her that the price of the gown is a small fraction of what will be spent on the day in total. If she isn't happy with her dress, the money she spends on photos will be wasted, since she won't like how she looks in them.

### "I like it, but I'm just not sure it's 'the one'."

Ask leading questions to determine what the bride's issues are with the gown, so you can identify what might be a better fit. Encourage her to try on additional dresses so she can feel confident she's looked at all alternatives. Sometimes it takes seeing a bunch of other dresses on to settle on the one she liked in the first place.

### "It's perfect, except for the sleeves/neckline/beading/etc."

Bring out some similar dresses in your sample collection without the offending feature. You can also find out if the feature she doesn't like can be changed — many custom-dress manufacturers will agree to customize gowns.

### "I saw a similar gown for much cheaper at the discount store/online/on eBay."

Point out the advantages to buying the gown in a full-service bridal boutique, such as on-site alterations or custom manufacturing. Note the quality of the merchandise (what she saw may be a cheap knock-off), any guarantees or refund policies offered, and your reputation as a reliable businessperson who delivers on promises. Ultimately it's up to them where they choose to shop, but with them in your store, you have the upper hand.

# 6.  Conclusion

*"The last seven years of my life with the boutique have been such a dream come true. I'm so glad I found the courage to do it. I love the work, I love my customers and I love my consignees."*

— Beverly, boutique owner

You have reached the end of the *FabJob Guide to Become a Boutique Owner*, but hopefully this is also the beginning of your journey to opening your own unique boutique. The rest of your education will come from talking to people in retail, reading and researching, and learning as you go. Included here are a few additional resources for expanding your knowledge of fashion and your retail know-how.

We wish you every success in your business venture and we look forward to discovering your unique boutique when we're out on the fashion prowl. Remember to believe in yourself and in the timeliness of pursuing your dream.

# Professional Associations and Groups

- *Association of Retail Marketing Services*
  **www.narms.com**

- *Footwear Distributors and Retailers of America*
  **www.fdra.org**

- *International Council of Shopping Centers*
  **www.icsc.org**

- *National Shoe Retailers Association*
  **www.nsra.org**

- *National Sporting Goods Association*
  **www.nsga.org**

- *Retail Loss Prevention Exchange*
  **www.rlpx.com**

# Trade Publications

- *Apparel News*
  **www.apparelnews.net**

- *The Apparel Strategist*
  **www.apparelstrategist.com**

- *Footwear News*
  **www.footwearnews.com**

- *Women's Wear Daily*
  **www.wwd.com**

- *Retailing Today*
  **www.retailingtoday.com**

- *Retail Traffic Magazine*
  **www.retailtrafficmag.com**

- *Stores Magazine*
  **www.stores.org**

- *Style.com*
  **www.style.com**

- *About.com About the Retail Industry*
  **http://retailindustry.about.com/od/abouttheretailindustry**

- *Sportswear International*
  **www.sportswearnet.com**

# Save 50% on Your Next Purchase

Would you like to save money on your next FabJob guide purchase? Please contact us at **www.FabJob.com/feedback.asp** to tell us how this guide has helped prepare you for your dream career. If we publish your comments on our website or in our promotional materials, we will send you a gift certificate for 50% off your next purchase of a FabJob guide.

# Get Free Career Advice

Get valuable career advice for free by subscribing to the FabJob newsletter. You'll receive insightful tips on: how to break into the job of your dreams or start the business of your dreams, how to avoid career mistakes, and how to increase your on-the-job success. You'll also receive discounts on FabJob guides, and be the first to know about upcoming titles. Subscribe to the FabJob newsletter at **www.FabJob.com/newsletter.asp**.

# Does Someone You Love Deserve a Dream Career?

Giving a FabJob® guide is a fabulous way to show someone you believe in them and support their dreams. Help them break into the career of their dreams with more than 75 career guides to choose from.

## Visit www.FabJob.com to order guides today!